Manna
For a Desert of Busyness

Praying Advent's Sunday Scripture

Joseph A. Tetlow, S.J.

Sheed & Ward

This book is for
A. Patrick Phillips,
Donald L. Gelpi, John R. Stacer,
and all of our companions
in the Society of Jesus

Sheed & Ward™ is a service of National Catholic Reporter Publishing Company, Inc.

Library of Congress Catalog Card Number:

ISBN: 1-55612-181-4

Published by: Sheed & Ward
               115 E. Armour Blvd. P.O. Box 419492
               Kansas City, MO 64141-6492

To order, call: (800) 333-7373

Contents

Third Sunday of Advent

Fourth Sunday of Advent

Christmas

Sunday after Christmas: The Holy Family

New Year's Day, The Solemnity of Mary

Epiphany of the Lord

Introduction

This is the second volume of *Manna for a Desert of Busyness,* a series of reflections on the three cycles of scripture readings for Sundays. This volume focuses on the readings assigned to Advent, as the first focused on those assigned to Lent. These reflections, too, are intended for men and women caught up in the busyness of postmodern life who want to deepen their interior life and perhaps find their way to prayer. Like the reflections in the earlier volume, these first put the Word of God and the works of our lifeworld in dialogue, then suggest some points for further consideration or discussion, and finally move into the kind of prayer which is direct address to God our Lord.

How can we get into interior prayer, those of us who trudge day after day through the spiritual dryness of career and job pressures, housework, family tensions, and a lifeworld threatening to fly apart? How can we wrap ourselves in the silence of God when we have to get to the bank or pick up the car, when one of the children is going through a phase, when the phone rings whenever it wants to, and when we do not quite understand the tensions flickering around our office? We have tried to take our lead from the wonderful women and men who dedicate their lives to contemplation in places like a convent of Poor Clares and the monastery at Gethsemani. We might have been being overly optimistic, and perhaps need to consider that the most appropriate form of prayer for someone working busily from the time they get up to the time they go back to bed will probably differ from the kind of prayer most appropriate for someone spending all day, every day in silence, recollection, study, and voluntary self-disciplines like fasting. The self-disciplines of those who live in the desert of busyness are not voluntary, and unless we pray, will seem more like deadening aggravations than the maturing penances they might be.

The fact is that very many laymen and laywomen, and very many pastors and religious, campus ministers and cursillistas, have set out to pray daily. They have wanted to achieve what we used to call mental prayer, or interior prayer, as opposed to liturgical prayer or vocal prayer with the rosary or from prayer books. So they have learned centering prayer from Basil Pennington, or prayer with the fantasy from Anthony de Mello, or contemplation from Thomas Greene or Henri Nouwen. And almost as-many as set out to pray in these contemplative modes—I am calling only on my own experience around the country—no longer pray every day. They no longer pray for the same kind of reason that many would-be athletes no longer exercise: they chose a kind of exercise that they almost surely could not continue, or began at a level of strenuousness that guaranteed burnout.

The most appropriate kind of prayer for mature Christians living in the desert of busyness is the prayer of consideration. This is the kind of praying that gave rise to the reflections in this book, and in turn, the reflections in this book are intended to lead back into the prayer of consideration. Every kind of prayer means the lifting of the mind and heart to God, but each kind of prayer does the lifting differently.

Very briefly, the prayer of consideration calls upon the strengths of reason and understanding, and upon the affectivity of those committed for others' sake to steady work and action. You do in this prayer just the same things you do when trying to understand why a woman wrote a will as she did so that you can apply its terms, or why the school's coaches cannot get along together so that you can help the school. You ask questions beginning with who, what, where, when, why and how: Who is it who does this? How could that have happened? What does this have to do with any experiences I have had? You do all this, of course, asking all along that you may be present to God as God is always present to you.

Most directly, the prayer of consideration applies to a statement or a document or a doctrine. You would consider, for example, the letters of St. Paul, or the elements in the Creed, or the Prologue to St. John's Gospel, or the Sermon on the Mount. You reason about them, ask God to help you understand them, and keep reflecting on your self, your life, and your lifeworld in the light of their truth. You could consider the doctrine of the Eucharist, as Thomas Aquinas did at great length, or you could consider what tradition tells you about justice, as Dorothy Day did.

You could also consider one of Jesus' parables as though it were not so much a story as a text. Who really is the prodigal son? What about the elder brother? Was Jesus actually talking about the father of the two—or His Father? Or again: Jesus told us to consider the lilies of the field, and then showed us how He prayed by sharing what He learned from them, Himself. *"Now if that is how God clothes the grass in the field, which is there today and thrown into the furnace tomorrow, will he not much more look after you, you people of little faith?"*

Finally, you can pray the prayer of consideration with Jesus' life as subject. This way differs from fantasizing, meditating, or contemplating, as the book's essays will show. We might just recall briefly what we already know of these ways of praying, to make sure we comprehend the appropriate way to pray with Scripture in the middle of a busy life.

Fantasy, first, allows us to be in God's presence while we fantasize things that have not and would not happen. You might fantasize yourself falling into the sun and coming to its still, incandescent center—and then change the fantasy and imagine that you have fallen into God, a furnace of creative love and of peace. Or you might fantasize that Jesus stands around and talks with you in your kitchen. This is a wonderful form of prayer for folk with strong imaginations.

Meditation—to take one of the ways it is talked about—means that in God's presence we remember vividly a real event by imagining it as it happened, perhaps in great detail and in exact sequence. For instance, you might sit very still in God's presence and in your mind visualize Jesus' birth. You might stand at the mouth of the cave and take in all the action, like a camera taking in movement and sound and even the atmosphere of the event. And then you fall into conversation with almighty God, or with one of the persons in the event.

Contemplation, in its turn, always involves being with Christ or with God. Sometimes you say a word or read a sentence in Jesus' life and then become completely absorbed in and by God the Lord, and you seem to do very little or even nothing at all; you are simply resting in God. That passive contemplation is a great gift from God. More active contemplation calls on the powers of the imagination and raises many images and feelings. In this kind of prayer, you really enter into an event in Jesus' life. The event is in the past to you, but all things are present in God and in God you enter into the event; you are there, hearing and seeing and feeling. You take part in what goes on—allowing Jesus to wash your feet, for instance, or taking the Infant from Mary. This kind of prayer goes beyond comprehension. The prayer itself is an experience, very real and as memorable as any other real event, and it freshens your affects and deepens your love of God and of others.

All three of these ways of praying demand considerable recollection during the whole day, and a kind of self-containment that many of us either do not feel called to or are truly prevented from reaching by the life God has called us to.

However busy we are, though, we can manage the prayer of consideration. Those who do it manifest a certain mature self-containment and are able to spend longish times alone. They also prove effective in setting aside a definite time and a definite place for their prayer.

They regularly find that two other activities help a great deal: first, reading those authors who stimulate us to reflection and prayer; and second, cultivating good friends to talk with about God and the church and our selves. Each of these activities is a kind of spiritual friendship.

The successive volumes of *Manna for a Desert of Busyness* are intended to be the kind of reading that moves us to the prayer of consideration. And we live in a time in the church's history when mature conversation about the things of God has come back into style. We really ought to thank God for that great gift by actively using it, and talking with spiritual friends.

I can testify from my own experience how greatly good friends help in the unfolding of a Christian's prayer life. I could go so far as to say that at least one Christian would not have a prayer life at all were it not for such good friends. So here I express my gratitude to the men whom God gave me as special companions since I was a teenager, the Jesuits who make up the Society of Jesus that I know. Some are dead: Anthony Mangiaracina, my first teacher, finished his life term; and Vicente Rodriguez, my greatest friend, was killed by the mistake of an American trooper in Santo Domingo. Some still teach me after long years: Ignatius M. Fabacher, Michael F. Kennelly, Joseph H. Fichter, George H. Raywood, Thomas H. Clancy. Some walk as my closest companions: A. Patrick Phillips, Donald L.Gelpi, John R. Stacer, Brian Zinnamon. Our conversation, a very great gift from the Spirit of God, often turns on the consideration of the Word of God and—we recognize this as an undeserved gift from God—*sets our hearts burning within us.*

Richard Rolle, a great English mystic who led an active life, wrote that his study of scripture had taught him this great truth: To love Christ Jesus above all else will entail three things: warmth and sweetness and song. Anyone who considers scripture as a member of a *priestly people* will come to know that warmth and sweetness and song. Anyone who considers the Word of God in this desert of busyness will come to know, too, how the same Spirit who gives its life to the living Word of God also gives us life in our lifeworld. To God be glory for ever and ever.

Joseph A. Tetlow, S.J.
Institute of Jesuit Sources
July 4, 1988

1. The Time Has Come

You know 'the time' has come. You must wake up now; our salvation is even nearer than it was when we were converted.

Jesus wanted to let His disciples know how He felt about all things, great and small. Once, He let them know how He felt about the endtime (Gospel). He sounded a little disconsolate as He said that when the Son of Man came again in glory, people would just be doing what they are always doing, *eating, drinking, taking wives, taking husbands.* That's what they were doing every time a cataclysm struck in the past. No reason to expect people to change; *as it was in Noah's day, so will it be when the Son of Man comes.*

Now, Jesus was talking about the Day of Judgment. *How mighty is that day—none like it,* to use Jeremiah's words. Jesus Himself had a vision of that last day in the endtime and must have felt awe at it. He hardly minced words talking about it.

However, Jesus was also talking about another day and another time: His own. For the Son of Man had already come and was walking around the face of the earth announcing Good News. God had personally entered into human history and begun the *last days.* That "time" had finally come, when God *chose to reveal the hidden plan God so kindly made in Christ from the beginning to act upon when the times had run their course to the*

1

end that God would bring everything together under Christ, as head, everything in the heavens and everything on earth.

Of that promised time, Jeremiah said, *"When the time comes, you will fully understand."* Well, the time has come, and we can very reasonably ask whether we *fully understand.* During Advent, we need to think about this time, the one that has already come, for it is as inescapable as the last day in the endtime and no human person can get away from the massive change that God has wrought.

Human history no longer clicks along like an Orient Express rolling west. It no longer follows a straight trajectory from the dawn of human life to the Last Day: amoeba, pseudopod, fish, pterodactyl, primate, human, Armageddon. Human life no longer unfolds solely from within itself, passed on from generation to generation, slowly developing the genetic code that geneticists begin to think took distinctive shape in a single woman's womb.

Instead, the true Beginning and End of human history and of humanity itself has leapt right into the middle of it and become its true center. "The Redeemer of Humankind," John Paul II wrote as the opening words of his first encyclical, "is the center of the universe and of history." Jesus Christ stands at the center of all that now lives and moves, of all that has lived and moved, and of all that ever will live and move.

His coming, then, definitively ended something and definitively began something. Before Jesus Christ, a great vacuum had whistled at the center of the whole groaning creation, at least as we know it on this globe of ours. As Paul explained it, sharing with the Romans his mystical vision of history's unfolding: *From the beginning till now the entire creation, as we know, has been groaning in one great act of giving birth.* Groaning, because the full birth kept not happening, and the vacuum at the center of creation redoubled its roar at each attempt. The reason, we now know: Human intelligence and freedom had been destined to be at that center, but for eons upon eons, human intelligence had not yet emerged. So *it was not for any fault on the part of creation that it was made unable to attain its purpose; it was made so by God,* who designed the world to reach the fullest expression of itself in human life and in humanity's dreaming and doing. We do not know exactly how many million years this little globe had endured before the earliest humans stood before God. Finally, they stood.

Stood—and promptly made things worse. Instead of filling with meaning and goodness the vacuum at the core of creation, we made the emptiness worse by annihilating the Godlife in us. We filled emptiness with nothingness—the evil of our sin and our guilt. We amplified its roar. For when we tried to put humanity at the center of all, we attempted to displace God.

None of us did this alone. We are so tightly grown together that each one implicated both self and others in this wickedness, all of us together banishing ourselves from the symphony of creation and leaving the earth without a functioning conductor. Century after tired century, the earth could only *hope to be freed from its slavery to decadence.* Humankind lost hope and jailed itself in iron laws of survival in the maelstrom of our own viciousness. During long centuries, we ate and made merry on our May Days, yet even as we celebrated, we needed a thousand forms of strong drink to anesthetize our hollowness.

And then *when the times had run their course to the end,* the saving time came. God *would bring everything together under Christ, as head, everything in the heavens and everything on earth.* To those whom He had chosen before any time began, He has revealed this, *for we have been anointed by the Holy One, and have all received this knowledge.*

What *knowledge?* Here are four thoughts.

We know "the time" has come (second reading). That's first: knowing. People seem always to be looking for a new age, a new order of things. Not Christians. We are as ready as anyone else to christen New Frontiers and New Beginnings, because that kind of politics is fun and sometimes even useful. But Christians know that *these are the last days* and that the last age has begun. We even know what that means: During this age, "God with us" does not mean merely that God will sort out human affairs to favor His friends and crush their enemies. Rather, in this last age, God means to favor all. *Emmanuel* has come into the very enspirited flesh that had so often seemed to humankind an enemy to fullness of life.

We are already living the *salvation that the prophets were looking and searching for so hard;* the prophecies that they *made were about the grace which was to come to you,* as Peter wrote in the very first papal encyclical. We are living an Advent, now completely *God's work of art,* as Paul put it for the Ephesians, *created in Christ Jesus to live the good life as from the beginning he had meant us to live it.*

Here is the second thought: We are now living exactly that *good life* that *from the beginning He had meant us to live. For "the time" had come* when Jesus was born to bring to fulfillment the tentative beginnings of life and mind and love on earth. The Father had always intended *to bring everything together under Christ as head.* The Creator's hope had projected a humankind willingly and joyfully accepting Christ as its head. But the Creator's hope found no scope among us that we would dwell peaceably among all other creatures, using them gently and deliciously and never abusing them. We no sooner came to freedom than we wrecked both our freedom and ourselves, and then started in on the earth.

That was the trajectory of history until Jesus of Nazareth. Then all trajectories decayed. Then, as Christ's disciples understand, a new humanness welled up from within this wrecked race. The source of this new humanness insures an eternal embodiment for each of us who *were baptized into His death... so that as Christ was raised from the dead by the Father's glory, we too might live a new life.*

Not so that we might live this new life later on, in the pale future. No; the time of that new life, that new humanness, has already come. We are not preparing for a new time and a new life. Each one of us prepares only for our full embodiment of this new life that we already live.

Consequently, third, *we know "the time" has come* when we are aware of living the future already in the present. The point here is as important as it is difficult. The life we now lead will alter and change, but not end and be started up again. We who now live will continue living, the same person, forever. This has tremendous impact on the way we comprehend our ordinary lives. For if we are to live the same person forever, then welling up from within this present life, from very deep within our actual selves, are desires and gifts meant by God to give shape to the future.

Were we able to let ourselves feel our deepest, most authentic desires, and were we able then to enact them—we would upon that instant inaugurate the Reign of God. We are setting aside here those who have authentically, willfully chosen self over against God and all others, those who are actively choosing self-will and an eternal loneliness. (We cannot explore the matter here, but in God's wisdom, somehow even they will always want to come into the Reign.) Counting all those who in however dim a way, however imperfectly, want to serve God, it goes this way: Suppose that each human person found out what he or she wants most of all, most deeply and most authentically. What would happen? Why, they would find out that they want most of all to live in Christ, to be children of God the Lord, to love one another with the love of the Spirit of God. That is, they would want most of all the Reign of God.

We do not make that arrangement of desires. God makes that arrangement of desires. Isaiah says that when he says (first reading) that the Lord God *will wield authority over the nations*. Here is how God will wield divine authority: Those who do not acknowledge Him, even those who now feel that they oppose Him, will in the end discover in their own selves the exulting desire to do precisely what God the Lord wants done.

Isaiah also noted (probably alluding to the same liturgical text as Hosea and Joel) that each one of the nations *will hammer swords into ploughshares*, willingly and even gleefully granting to all other peoples what each people wants for itself. Each nation is to come to desire this on its own now, for this is the age during which *the ministry of reconciliation* between God and humankind has been entrusted to humankind.

Hence, we also know that humankind must finish what Jesus of Nazareth began under the Spirit of the Lord. We are *to bring good news to the poor, to proclaim liberty to captives and to the blind new sight, to set the downtrodden free, to proclaim the Lord's year of favor*. We know that we are to root out every practice, notion, or fad that diminishes human dignity and freedom, or stands in the way of a wholehearted yes to Jesus-Christ. We are not meant to spend our lives absorbed in a struggle against peccadilloes, or even worse, absorbed in self-centered sinful foolishness. Our destiny lies on the broadest horizon.

Here we have God's project for the saints still on earth, what we are sent by God to do in the meantime, while waiting for the endtime. We who are mature disciples are summoned to grow in the wisdom that discerns from among all our desires and gifts those that have been established by God the Creator as the structure of the completed kingdom. These holy desires and gifts are already grown into our living; we are to name them and regenerate them in others.

Here is the fourth and final thought. *We know "the time" has come* when God the Lord has made Himself every human person's absolute future. Beyond time, beyond our native capacities, beyond what we think could make us happy—God has chosen to stand as the One toward whom we grow. Whether any of us has another tomorrow or not, all of us have this future *as adopted children and co-heirs with Jesus Christ: Eternal life,* which is this, *to know you, the only true God.*

This is our actual destiny. The Father seized us before we could argue with Him and *stamped us with the seal of the Holy Spirit of Promise,* making Himself that toward which our days move us along, making His divine Son the Omega point into whom our humanity wakes up dawn by dawn.

We are up against the *mysterium fidei* here, so we had better talk a little more precisely, at least in one particular. For the truth is not that we go towards God; the truth is that God comes towards us. For this reason we say over and over at Mass that "we wait in joyful hope for the coming of our Lord and Savior Jesus Christ." We wait. We are at every instant wholly present to Him, and known utterly for what we are. He must choose the ways to be present to us, and makes Himself known insofar as He wishes, to each one of us and to all of us. Our central task—the definition of all our tasks—is to wait.

To us, it doesn't matter whether Paul was alluding to the parousia or not when he wrote that *"The 'time' has come."* Each of us lives a little human history, and *we know "the time" has come already,* right into the middle of it.

We believe, then, that we know the true course of human history. We might ask whether we live like people who guard a tremendous, happy secret.

How can our Salvation lie at the center of our lifeworld and even of our selves, when we are the ones who need saving?

At the Last Judgment, God will not weigh acts and merits heaped over a lifetime. God will read the message we have written deep in our self.

Prayer

Lord Jesus Christ
Lord of all realms and of all histories,
We acknowledge You Beginning and End.
We confess You the Center
through whom all things are coming to be.
Summoning all our freedom,
there we place You in our own lives.

We want our desires to rise out of Your desires,
our hopes to reflect Your hopes
for our own selves and for all humankind.
For we know, Mighty God,
that Your wish is our peace,
Your project, the salvation of every man and woman.

We praise You, Lord Jesus Christ,
for Your faithful love and for Your victory.
In You we place all our trust, saying to You
Now that the time has come:

To my Lord I give each hour of my life.
To my God, the use of all my days
and the seal of my death.

For You are Lord for ever and ever. Amen.

2. Hilarious Story

You do not know when the master of the house is coming—evening, midnight, cockcrow, dawn.

Jesus often encouraged His friends to live mindful of God's steady presence in their lives. He did not want them to live so preoccupied with ordinary things that they would advert to God only on the Sabbath. Sometimes He told them bluntly, "Be on your guard," or "Stay awake!" Sometimes, He told parables or made comparisons.

Once, He compared our situation to that of a group of servants. Their master went off for the evening, perhaps to a symposium or a party from which he might *come back evening, midnight, cockcrow, dawn.* Before setting out, *he had told the doorkeeper to stay awake* (Gospel). In fact, he had desired all of the servants to watch for their master's return.

Jesus used this little incident to illustrate our tendency to slacken our attention and let it drift. He was characterizing us, the servants of the Lord. *"So stay awake, because you do not know when the master of the house is coming"* (Gospel). Jesus gave no indication that He intended to characterize the master. For instance, nothing suggests that the master willfully left his return ambiguous, or that the master was crassly putting his people to some kind of test.

Our tendency, in homily and catechism and even in books of spiritual discourse, has been to go beyond Jesus' point. With a sense of dread and awe, we create a rather tough image of this "master of the house" and then project that image onto God our Creator and Lord. We use considerable imagination to make God seem like some of the masters all of us have known—self-centered, unpredictable, willful, little concerned with our comfort or security. We let our guilt-rusted fantasies go, and project a God carrying on like a headachy tyrant fuming around court late Friday afternoon. We make God like Shakespeare's Prospero, tricking friend and enemy with cruel illusions.

Well, we are making all that up. Jesus drew no such portrait. The mere fact that we so readily make God "the master of the house" suggests that we still entertain odd notions about the God *named our Redeemer forever* (first reading).

We need to scotch such odd notions any time they arise, but the beginning of Advent offers a particularly productive occasion. For during Advent we think constantly about salvation history, and it is into our understanding of salvation history that we weave the oddest possible notions about God.

No surprise there: We have odd notions of salvation history. See if the following does not capture the way many Christians imagine the story of God's work in the world, when they give it any thought at all.

Almighty God established His decrees in eternity and then created the world. Right off, humankind chomped into some delicious fruit that God had forbidden it. Being infinitely just, God had to drive the sinners away and to clang shut behind them the gates of holiness and wholeness. For He was infinitely offended by the sin, and would have to demand infinite punishment and infinite satisfaction. All this happened around 50,000 B.C. or 200,000 B.C., depending on the latest Carbon-10 tests on archeological jaw bones.

Then around 5,000 B.C., the Spirit of God persuaded the Creator to try to save a remnant. Humanity was evolving satisfactorily in some ways but was clearly heading for further floods. Various mostly naked peoples worshiped animals, trees, mountains. Others, like the Greeks, began wearing clothes, writing on tablets, inventing salacious fables about gods, and worshiping statues. Too many offered blood sacrifices to strange gods, all too often with one another's blood.

So around this time the Spirit led Abram out of Chaldea. Unhappily, Abraham sired a people who turned out practically as wicked as anyone. They killed all the prophets and then became hypocrites. Even Isaiah, who never hesitated to tell God exactly what was on his mind, had to admit to the Lord that *You have delivered us up to our own guilt* (first reading).

Around 2,000 B.C., the Son went to the Father as humankind's advocate and asked God to relent. But the Father could not act contradictorily. Because He was truly just, He could not accept to be propitiated until the decrees He had made were perfectly obeyed and infinite satisfaction was made for the offenses against His infinite wisdom. The Son suggested, "I will go down to the earth and as a human obey Your will perfectly." The Father was not notably enthusiastic. What about restitution? Justice demands not only that things be put right again, but that satisfaction be made for former injustices. Then the Son said, all right, He would take upon Himself all of humanity's debt and burden and suffer for all of it, going through real death. No faking? No; real, bloody death. After all, if the Father had been propitiated temporarily by the blood of bulls and goats, then He could not reasonably refuse to be completely, permanently propitiated by the real blood of His own Son. And that holy blood would pay humanity's full debt to the Father, being of infinite worth.

As we know, in 1 B.C. the Father finally agreed, and *the Word was made flesh*, inaugurating 1 A.D. In the flesh, *He is the sacrifice that takes our sins away, and not only ours, but the whole world's*, as John wrote in his first letter.

That ends the narrative.

Isn't this the way some otherwise wonderfully sane disciples of Jesus Christ believe? The narrative would be hilarious except for two things. First, too many believe something very close to it. And second, they are believing a narrative that skirts the blasphemous and yet contains fragments of the truth (that's the way of heresies).

One monstrous error, however, lies under the shards of truth: This god bears only a surface resemblance to the God of Jesus Christ. Could the god of this story say of Jesus, *"Here is my servant whom I uphold, my chosen one in whom my soul delights,"* as Yahweh says in Isaiah's First Servant Song? Hardly. He sounds rather like the kind of father whom Jesus scorned, *who would hand his son a stone when he asked for bread, or a snake when he asked for a fish.*

No, the Father of that not-so-hilarious narrative is not Jesus's Father. Anyone who hesitates to say so needs to hear a relevant bit of Israel's belief about and practice of expiatory sacrifice.

In their early days as a people, those who sprang from Abraham's loins and Sarah's womb appear not to have offered any sacrifice at all to Yahweh. So Isaiah puts these words into Yahweh's mouth: *"I did not exact from you the service of offerings, nor weary you for your frankincense."* As time went on, though, they noticed the folk around them offering sacrifices to their gods. They at first listed that as one more practice that would dishonor the God of gods. Their own more typical sacrifice, decreed in Deuteronomy, was to offer a tithe of all their produce *to the Levite, the stranger, the orphan and the widow,* as a gift back to God of all *"you, Yahweh, have given me."* Time went on, though, and the people began finding different meanings in religious symbols and symbolic actions. They gradually adopted the practice of their neighbors; they began offering to the God of Hosts grain in thanksgiving and the lives of animals as expiation for their infidelities.

Yet from the start, they realized that they could do nothing to buy God's mercy, nothing to make God be merciful. They could not begin to assuage His raging grief at the hurts they inveterately visited upon themselves, not even by offering rivers of blood and mountains of first fruits. In one of the more mysterious shifts in human thinking, they realized that God Himself does the expiating. *"For the sake of my name I deferred my anger, for the sake of my honor I curbed it; I did not destroy you."* God sets right the disorder of sin; we cannot do that. God breaks the iron links between the sinner's sin and the calamities consequent upon it; we can only suffer them. God the Lord moved spontaneously to save the people, as the prophets kept reminding them. So Isaiah: *"It is I, I, who wipe out, for my own sake, your offenses; your sins I remember no more."*

Now we are approaching the truer narrative. God who saves, *God named our redeemer forever,* came into our enspirited flesh and lives in our humanness now and forever. This God is no absentee landlord. This God does not go off for an indefinite period of time, like the master of the household did in Jesus' illustration. That is quite unthinkable. Having risen from the dead and come again into our enspirited flesh, the Word of God lives in it forever. He *is our life itself,* as Paul wrote to the Colossians, *our wisdom, our righteousness and sanctification and redemption.*

We must be very careful not to imagine that our sin comes first, and then God plans what to do about it. Our sins are indescribably ineffectual before God, who did not wait upon our silliness and our viciousness to envision and to hope. God's action in the world does not begin with redemption, after sin. Very much the contrary; God's action in the world begins with constant creation which, after sin, transmutes into salvation.

In the deep reaches of eternity and of infinite love, the Persons who are God fill their mutual life with every possible love. Like the light and heat of our sun, which spill out riotously from the sun as it implodes upon itself in total intensity, that love spills out riotously from God. The Creator keeps creating—worlds, cycles, persons—all that actually exists, not merely new creatures coming to be. For did the Creator stop creating, all that is would no longer be.

Of all creatures, He chooses to create some who can in their measure return to their Creator the most precious gift the Creator gives to them, love. So God creates humankind full of desires to know and to be known, to give self and to accept the gift of self, all in great, if circumscribed, freedom. This means, somehow, that each human person reflects love to the Father the way the Son reflects it. We come from God as from a parent; were turn to God as siblings and God's children.

Being everywhere present and always in the present, God knew how we would fail ourselves, one another, and God's own project. The Creator's choice: Sin will not prevent Me.

Here is the truer narrative, embodied in a most ancient hymn recorded in the letter to the Colossians: *He is the image of the unseen God and the first-born of all creation, for in him were created all things in heaven and on earth.... As he is the Beginning, he was first to be born from the dead, so that he should be first in every way.* Because Jesus Christ lives *the fullness of divinity,* He has all power in heaven and earth; and because He loves humankind with infinite tenderness, *He has overridden the Law, and canceled every record of the debt that we had to pay.* That was His choice. And He has done it.

The Greek words for propitiate, expiate, make gracious and cause to be merciful—all are closely connected to the root of another word: hilarious.

If we grasp the true narrative of God's spontaneous expiation of our sins, we will have hold of a story that is, in every radical meaning of the word, hilarious.

What is it about us that we imagine our sin comes first and God's choice to redeem comes only after that?

What makes us imagine that God the Creator could act vindictively?

We can live a joy-filled life on no other grounds than these, that God is achieving His loving purposes. Our happiness lies precisely in letting God come when He will come.

Prayer

Whether You come to us, God our Father,
evening, midnight, cockcrow, dawn,
You come caring and in tender love.

For out of Your own unmeasurable goodness
You have elected to brush aside our sin,
refusing to lose us whom You chose to love
though in our blundering we throw ourselves away.

Yet we cling to images of You
angry, furious, vindictive, unforgiving.
Do not be offended, Father,
we do not mean to offend
when we project our ugly fantasies upon You.
For we act under the fear of our own shadows
the shadows of our many failures
the shadow of our death.

And as we wait here in weltering disorder
we act out our anxiety that You might not come in time.

Eternal and always loving Father,
We protest from our deepest hearts
we believe that You do come in time and never fail.

And You have already marked the day
and the morning, noon, or night,
when You will come to save us,
Because You have so chosen,
Because You are mighty God
and Lord of all
forever and ever. Amen.

3. Standing Secure

Stand secure before the Son of Man.

While we celebrate Advent, we seem to be looking backward and forward at the same time. We stand in a time like an uncertain Spring day, whose cold winds could blow it right back into winter, but whose bright sun could warm it quickly into summer. Advent is like that, and we stand unsure whether we are supposed to be appreciating the past or getting girded up to take on the future.

Our most obvious preparation follows the church's very ancient practice. We are preparing to celebrate the historical event of Jesus' birth. We will remember that birth actually happening on an ordinary day in Bethlehem of Judah—well, on a mildly chaotic day during an imperial census, but ordinary enough in an occupied country. We will recall our belief that God has fulfilled His promise *to raise up for David a just shoot.*

We get ready to remember, however, by reading the prophets. In them, we hear announced the coming of the Messiah along with the coming of the *Son of Man in glory.* That is, we find consistently connected and intertwined Jesus' first coming and His second coming.

As a consequence, during Advent we look backward and forward at the same time. We can get confused. For a review of God's promises does not just console us with God's work in the past and send us into the dim warmth of the creche. It also confronts us with the dark of the future, including *the coming of the Lord Jesus Christ with all His holy ones.* Not only that, but the prophets' projections of this Second Coming do not leave us feeling warm and snug in any way.

In fact, Jesus' own scenario—the reading from Luke is just a snippet of the whole, and there remain the fearsome lines of Matthew's twenty-fifth chapter—depicts some awesome happenings. *Nations will be in anguish,* convulsed in war and revolution. Peoples will thrash about *distraught.* Events will reach such a pitch *that men will die of fright in anticipation of what is coming upon the earth.*

Anyone with a moderate imagination can feel knee-thews turning to hot wax on hearing the descriptions. Jesus certainly did not give more encouragement than we need when He told us, *"When these things begin to happen, stand erect and hold your heads high, for your deliverance is near at hand."* We might be inclined to feel that unless our deliverance is near enough to actually hold us up, we will very probably be found flat on our faces.

Well, after centuries of trial and error and correction, the church has grown very wise. We know we cannot contemplate life's harsh things for long and not get disconsolate unless we alternate to contemplating life's lovely things from time to time. We can hope a little more easily that we will *stand secure before the Son of Man* when He comes to separate the sheep from the goats if we position ourselves before His crib as well as before His throne.

That's the work of Advent, particularly, though the entire church year keeps us at it. In this season, we stand back and gaze into the past and into the future, contemplating the entire course of salvation history.

Are we arrogant, to think that we know the whole course of human history? We can go around and around on this, but what has been handed down to us could hardly be clearer: *God has given us the wisdom to understand fully the mystery, the plan He was pleased to decree in Christ,* Paul told the Ephesians. Jesus Himself said to His disciples, *"To you the mystery of the reign of God has been confided."*

That mystery and plan is not an abstraction, an $E = mc2$. We do not know it in theory. We do not know it the way we know about the battles of Alexander or the dates of the Roman emperors, our heads stuffed full of dry fact and suspiciously exact dates. We know *the mystery, the plan* in— even as—the actual events of our own lives. Our gift of faith turns out to be a gift of a way of knowing, so that when we look back into our own lives, we know God's infinite power breaking into human history.

We are like the sacristan in Chicago who was about to throw out an old, dented chalice. Someone insisted that he have it appraised by art experts, and he made a startling discovery. The chalice was hundreds of years old, probably the oldest of all the sacred vessels that Christians have preserved. The chalice is in a museum now, and everyone who sees it knows what they are looking at. The sacristan, who had gazed at it enough times to grow tired of it, simply did not know what he was looking at. Neither do we, too many times, when we look at the little history that is our own lives.

Most of us look back over our lives only reluctantly, perhaps to go to confession or for therapy. But we have the right willingly to recall what *His power at work in us* has accomplished, to praise Him for it. We are grounded in the present moment just exactly the way we were grounded in each past moment, and just the way we will be grounded in every coming moment—in God's own passionately creative love. We work and wonder with an energy whose ultimate source is not locked in subatomic particles, but flows free in the One who is more intimate to atoms than are their particles and surpasses the reaches of the universe even if this creation is somehow infinite. We grow and increase from a secret inside source linked with the most public outside source, a Spirit of Life who goes before and will come after. *In Him we live and move and have our being.*

Most of us look forward even more reluctantly than we look back, at least beyond doing some reasonable financial planning and some medium-range career and family planning. We suffer not only through a denial of death; we take every cosmetic means available to disguise even our ageing. We just do not particularly like looking carefully at our own future. Of course, we know perfectly well, even as we lay up for ourselves earthly treasure, *that moths and rust corrode; thieves break in and steal,* and none of it will last forever. We know all that; we just prefer not to think about it.

Then along comes Advent, when the church intervenes, arresting with the scriptures and the prayers our reluctance to look both backward and forward. During this season, while we are connecting our past with our future, we ought to keep three brief points in mind.

First, we are not engaged in an exercise in nostalgia. All well and good that the cast iron figures of the creche in St. Louis's classical old cathedral on the banks of the Father of Waters are the oldest figures west of that mighty river. Splendid that a family sets up a crib that five generations have cherished. That's important and beautiful, but must not mask what we are truly remembering.

We are not engaged in another kind of nostalgia, the kind that hankers for life in another—obviously, more beautiful and orderly—time. Nowhere in Advent does the church express the wish that those of us now alive could have lived when Jesus lived. For the mature disciple, adoration at the creche is not a longing to be back there. It is a longing to grow into Christ now in our flesh. Each human equally shares humanity with Jesus, though we are far from living lives which show plainly our wish to "share in His divinity who did not hesitate to share in our humanity." We have much still to do. So, no nostalgia.

Then, second, we are not remembering our people's and our own past as a kind of therapy. God knows there are quite enough traumas to ventilate: golden calves, inquisitions, anti-popes, the abounding stupidities about ethnic origins and skin colors. And any one of us can name sins that make us burn with shame. We do not, however, name them and hold them up to the bright present air in order to shake out musty repressions and stubborn anxieties. Our purpose extends well beyond that.

We name all the healed and half-annealed sins of the past, and all the little tactical and great strategic victories, in order *to wait in joyful hope*. Our work in remembering things past is powered by the energies of faith. We want to recognize throughout the past the faithfulness of the One who says, *"I will fulfill the promise I made,"* and who has been powerfully sustaining us in both greenwood and dry.

Finally, third, Christians do not remember things of our past as though these things were merely past, over and done with. For we remember with the mind of Christ, who has the mind of God, and to God all is now. This is not easy to understand, but the anamnesis in the Mass—the passage in which we recall the Last Supper, and the central event of consecration—gives us a paradigm. *"Do this, remembering Me."* Our obedience to Christ's command to consecrate and share makes actual what God promised. The Lord Jesus Christ comes back to His disciples, present in symbol and in truth.

Plainly, our own free obedience could not achieve that. Our own memory has no such power. Yet we go on *doing this* and much else that He commanded us, and the church has evolved, like Paul, *impelled by that energy of His which is so powerful a force within me.* When we acknowledge in our selves *that mystery hidden from ages and generations past but now revealed to His holy ones,* we shuck off the past as burden and cannot be cowed by the uncertainties of the future. We bow neither backward nor forward, but stand up straight.

We *stand secure before the Son of Man,* lying in the crib and seated on the throne.

This all suggests that a disciple of Jesus Christ looks on the past differently from those who do not believe. And on the future, too.

In the end, it seems a great favor that, as long as we stand in God's love, whatever we remember of the past secures our future for us.

What could come to pass in the future that God has not mastered in the past, even in our own lives?

Prayer

We praise You, Lord God,
that You summon us to stand in Your presence
and to serve You
out of the tangle of all we remember,
in the welter of all we have learned to desire.

We praise You, Lord God,
that You encompass the past and all that is in it
holding in Your own heart
all our yesterdays and all the aeons gone before them.

We praise You, Lord God,
that You already reach the future
going always on before what is to come
and there beyond when we arrive in our tomorrows.

We praise You, Lord God,
that You Yourself are always wholly present
to Yourself, to all the earth, to each of us.
We praise You that You call us into life out of chaos.
We praise You that You attend to us swamped in need.
We praise You that in the completeness of Your own love
You choose to love us.

We praise You, Lord God, and we worship You,
who always have been and ever will be
in realms without end.   Amen.

4. The Day of the Lord

"Who warned you to fly from the retribution that is coming?"

When we hear today about "retribution," we tend to think of an uncomfortably hot place where each one of us will be punished for our personal sins. We are influenced in this by the individualism of our age, which gives us the tendency to see everything in personal terms. We are also influenced by the word itself.

"Retribution" once meant any kind of recompence at all, but now refers to divine punishment, and mostly to divine punishment in the world to come.

That is too bad, because the shift in meaning lessens the force of this prophecy and of many like it: *"Who warned you to fly from the retribution that is coming?"* John the Baptist and other prophets were not talking about the world to come. They were talking about what was inexorably coming to the world: the Day of the Lord.

The "Day of the Lord"?

The very first prophetic book, the Book of Amos, announces the theme already current among the people. The elders conceived of it as a glorious, cataclysmic event, the coming of Yahweh at the head of their armies to defeat all their overwhelmingly more powerful enemies. They believed

21

that God would at that time make them understand everything about their own history, and fill their everyday lives with meaning.

During the bad times, the people kept up hope that the Day of the Lord would come and vindicate God's people. Ezekiel, for instance, promised during their servitude in Babylon that the Day of the Lord would mark *the end of an epoch.* Instead of living in captivity under their enemies, the people would rule over all of them. A couple of generations earlier, Jeremiah had dodged Nebuchadnezzar's soldiery around the occupied territory of Judea promising that the Lord would *send winnowers to Babylon to winnow her and leave her country bare in the day of disaster.* Both prophets wrote in gloomy times to say that God would seize dominion over all other powers in the Day of the Lord. Joel, who wrote prophetic liturgies of lamentation for people standing in fields stripped bare by a plague of locusts, promised that God Himself will come to *restore the fortunes of Judah and Jerusalem.*

But once the people's fortunes had been restored, once they were free to govern themselves and their silos were stuffed with grain, the people grew diffident about Yahweh. In the good times, they even grew unfaithful. Then the prophets began projecting a different image of the Day of the Lord.

Obadiah, for instance, had to remind them that the Day of the Lord *was near for all the nations,* including Israel. For God would judge Israel right along with all the rest of the nations, and perhaps with a more stringent measure. *As you have done, so will it be done to you; your deeds will recoil on your own head.* During those times when the people proved completely unfaithful to Yahweh and worshiped false gods instead, prophets began to sound like the "prophets" we know, vividly, starting with Amos: Trouble for those who are waiting so longingly for the Day of Yahweh! *What will this day of Yahweh mean for you? It will mean darkness, not light, as when a man escapes a lion's mouth only to meet a bear.*

We should notice here a parallel in our own lives. When a disciple gets really careless and starts living a life of sin, then the Day of the Lord will loom threateningly. God Himself will seem a hideous strength, holding back a devastating blow only with difficulty. We should recognize this for what it is: one of the ways God deals with the faithless. We have to recognize that this kind of fear of God tells us very little about the Lord, and a great deal about the way of life of the one who fears.

On the other hand, when we are really trying to stay away from sin, then the Day of the Lord will promise to come like an alleluia. We will still feel fear of the Lord—but this fear marks *the beginning of wisdom,* and tells us a good deal about the Lord of Hosts who *is mighty God,* and at least this little about wise persons, that they recognize their creaturehood.

Have the disciples of Jesus Christ to fear the Day of the Lord? We have a tendency today to hold fear and terror at arm's length, including fear of God and terror at the thought of Hell. We may need to recall that Jesus Himself and the apostles often called up the older image. The writer of the Second Epistle of Peter, for instance, drew a starkly vivid picture of the parousia (probably because after the Fall of Jerusalem people wondered whether the parousia would ever come). It will, the writer said in the climax of his letter. Indeed, believe that it will come: *the heavens will be destroyed in flames and the elements will melt away in a blaze. What we await are new heavens and a new earth where, according to his promise, the justice of God will reside.* Paul was content to point out, as he did to the Thessalonians, that this Day would come upon them *like a thief;* but John depicts in his Book of Revelations a wild scene of cosmic battle between demons and angels.

For all that, we have to make sure that the glare of the cosmic imagery does not wipe out the steady light we have already been given. For we know that when Jesus talked about *"My day,"* He did not refer to something yet to come. He referred to the very day He was then living, and also to the age He had inaugurated: *"Your father Abraham rejoiced that he might see my day. He saw it and was glad."* In a very real sense, we already live in the Day of the Lord. So even though the disciples of Christ keep before our minds the Old Testament image of the Day of the Lord coming in the endtime, we have our own understanding of this Day, more appropriate to the last of all ages. We believe simply that *God never meant us to experience the Retribution.*

John the Baptizer had announced this new Day of the Lord even as Jesus came into public view. At the Jordan, it is true, he used a great number of images that belong to the apocalyptic tradition, images that display the power and might of God at work, *winnowing, clearing the threshing floor, gathering His grain, burning chaff in unquenchable fire.* But John perceived God doing all this right there, each day he proclaimed his message as the precursor. He saw judgment going on right in front of his eyes. For although his own baptism was a cleansing meant to symbolize readiness to repent and to put on the fresh garments of righteousness, John saw plainly that the One to come *will baptize you in the Holy Spirit and fire,* which would mean entering into new life.

That baptism in the Spirit, John implied, would inaugurate the Day of the Lord. That is the baptism that each one of us has received. So we are not waiting for some titanic battle still to come. The really ultimate battle has already happened, on a low knoll outside of Jerusalem. To the powers of darkness whom it routed, the battle was humiliatingly small and appeared insignificant. To us whom it glorified, it was humiliatingly small and transcendently significant. We embrace its humiliation in the One humiliated; we are embraced by the Victor's transcendent power. For the time being, we also embrace its humiliating smallness as we simply going through a daily struggle, each of us trying to get free enough of the rubble left by the battle to accept the victory in joy.

The judgment established by that battle's outcome goes on moment by moment, as Jesus said: *"Whoever rejects me and does not accept my words already has his judge, namely, the word I have spoken—it is that which will condemn him on the last day."* For those who accept Jesus Christ live in Him just the way branches live in a vine. When the time comes for harvest, they will as a matter of course be taken up into life, just as those who have been cut off from Him will be thrown elsewhere, also as a matter of course. The course has been set; the lives of individuals go forward under the judgment of the Word that we have heard.

Well, this takes us back to where we began. We have to take John's warnings personally and individually after all. We must be able to know whether we are accepting Jesus Christ or not; we must have some kind of awareness whether we are living according to His Word. Not only John the Baptizer, but the Spirit of Life queries us: *Who told you to fly from the retribution that is coming?*

This is very sober business. Do any of us live as though fleeing the merciful pressures of God's Word? We do not deal here with trivialities or with externals merely. We are questioning whether any one of us lives crosswise to his or her own conscience, in important matters. That's fleeing, getting out from under, repudiating the living Word of God in us since we were *baptized in the Holy Spirit and in fire.* Any such attempt is doomed to failure, though the failure might not be very visible or vivid before the final Day of the Lord. On that day, however: wide screen, technicolor, stereo, three-dimensional.

For the rest, we do not live on tiptoe as though we were trying to see over every day to the big jubilee just beyond the horizon. We walk fairly flat-footed, doing what we can to respond to John's admonition: *"Give some evidence that you mean to reform."*

Now we come to the reason why prophets, holy writers, and homilists (in a certain vein) tend to whip up the Day of the Lord in holy froth. *Reform? Evidence of reform?*

The noonday devil in us reasons that we who practice our religion have of course matured in our faith and of course live a continuing reform of life. We can very easily get to acting like those other religious folk who ambled down to Jordan in their robes and tassels to look in on the commotion and to let the people see them. With them, we would explain to John that we are truly repentant and do habitually reform our lives. John snaps back, *"If you are repentant, produce the appropriate fruit."*

Here, finally, is what those of us who live the Day of the Lord really need to hear. *Produce the appropriate fruit.* It is not enough for us that we "do nothing wrong." That is no way to run an orchard, just keeping rot out of the trees. We have clearly to be doing things that are right, because *"any tree that fails to produce good fruit will be cut down,"* as Jesus told His disciples. And any branch that bears no fruit *"will be cut off."*

Strong stuff. What does this racy kind of language really mean, though, day to day?

A great deal. It means that if any of us does not get more patient as the days go by, more compassionate with those around, then we are not producing fruit. It means that we gradually learn to give more and more presents and gifts, sacrificing more and more of our own convenience and pleasure in order to do it. It means in our day a growing ability and liking for self-revelation to spouse, intimates, and friends. It means making friends of our children and of their children—never making them feel disgust. And so through the most mundane of human things: Pray as Jesus did, thanking and asking. Live chastely, not lunging after carnal pleasure. Tell the truth whenever. Help the poor as Paul got the Corinthians and the Galatians to do, *not grudgingly as though made to,* but more and more trustingly and openly, *for God loves a cheerful giver.* Like the not-very-likeable.

This kind of *evidence that we mean to reform* seems hardly startling. Yet, did we all live the great Good News of the new commandment as the Spirit teaches us in our hearts, we would live startlingly different lives. Some people around us might find the spectacle even more edifying than this one, yet to come (first reading): *The wolf lives with the lamb, the panther lies down with the kid; calf and lion cub feed together, with a little boy to lead them.*

That is how we are meant to live already in this Day of the Lord.

In the face of all this, we have to believe that each of us can know surely whether the course we have set will take us into joyful light when judgment comes, or into woeful shadows.

When we remember the final judgment, we are faced with the question whether we may not be concentrating so intensely on righting injustices among us to live forgetful of the final righting of all injustices.

In that forgetfulness, we may have domesticated the vast forces competing in and for the human spirit—forces far beyond what any one of us can manage.

Prayer

Deliver us, Lord,
still standing among us,
from the cataclysms we prepare to drop on ourselves.

Deliver us, Lord Jesus,
for we know that God the all-just
will not be deceived,
and where we resist Your Spirit's guiding,
there our just Judge will note default,
and hold us answerable
where we have no answer to give.

Deliver us, Lord,
Shepherd of our souls,
through the Word spoken in us
when we were baptized in the Spirit
and in the fire of divine love.

Deliver us, Lord Jesus Christ,
or who will deliver us from the threat
that we are to our own selves
and from the retribution that we wilfully ripen
in our own sins?

Deliver us.
We know You will deliver us.
For we cannot find it in ourselves
to fear Your coming again in might and glory
whom we have known as merciful King
and Shepherd wonderfully watchful of Your flock.

Praise be to You, Lord Jesus Christ.
Maranatha!
Come, Lord Jesus!

5. Finding God's Way

Prepare a way for the Lord.

As do people in every other language, we English-speakers use the word "way" to name a lot more than a road or a route. We talk about the way to cook stew and the way somebody eats it. We say a sick friend's in a bad way, an eccentric friend's got peculiar ways, a sailing friend's boat makes way. We still occasionally talk about the pagans' ways, though we have mostly forgotten that early in our history people called Christianity The Way.

We all talk this way (there it is), naming things with which we are easy and familiar. But we know one "way" with which we are not always easy and familiar. At least, when we come to one of its turnings, we have to concentrate, remember, and sometimes puzzle. For as Isaiah reported: *"My thoughts are not your thoughts, my ways not your ways—it is Yahweh who speaks."*

But God's way is marked with definite signs at every turning. Here are five that will help us recognize it. They will bring us to a conclusion that might just as well be stated now: To prepare a way for God in our lifeworld, we have to begin deep in our own hearts.

First of the five marks of God's way: It is a saving way, never a destroying way. It is true that when God *contemplated the earth, it was*

28

corrupt, for corrupt were the ways of all flesh on the earth. It is true that *His heart grieved at it,* and He let the dire and hideous consequences of sin pour down upon humankind. He let them flood human existence almost back into the unconsciousness from which He had graciously called it forth. But it is also true that God does not snuff out and start over. His most punishing corrections of those whom He loves are like a flood that washes and subsides rather than wipes out.

That is what makes one of the first symbols of God's covenants—the rainbow—so clear and accurate. After the adventures of the flood had all subsided, God made a covenant with Noah and told him: *"When the bow appears in the clouds, I will recall the covenant between myself and you and every living creature.... The waters shall never again become a flood to destroy all things of flesh."* The rainbow is a perfect symbol of God's covenant fidelity: so surprising and beautiful a light, barely to be believed, the rainbow appears after the earth has been saved from both drought and deluge.

That should comfort us, who live in a world in which the very things that we make to keep ourselves secure turn to threaten us. We need to remember the rainbow when stockpiled weapons rattle and when we take an account that our nation spends enough on atomic submarines to wipe from the entire world all of childhood's communicable diseases.

God's way, second, is life. He is *the living God* whose Spirit breathes across fields of dead bones bringing them to life. He is *the God of the living, not of the dead,* as Jesus told the Sadducees when trying to help them understand resurrection. Once God raises a living enspirited flesh, God does not allow that flesh to perish. *"Do not be afraid, Jacob, poor worm, Israel, puny mite. I will help you—the Holy One of Israel is your Redeemer."*

This is important to us. Humankind keeps giving itself to various servitudes; we now recognize, for instance, that smoking and drinking are more than habits, they are addictions that lay upon a population like a plague. They—and many other customs in our culture—somehow "enslave" us. Yet we keep inflicting these various servitudes on one another.

Even as we do, God leads—*Yahweh alone is [Israel's] guide.* However set we seem to be on wrecking ourselves, God leads Israel out of Egypt and out of Babylon and out of everything internecine and *makes an everlasting covenant* with us, determined that *"you shall be my people and I shall be your God."*

We are incredibly fortunate that God has chosen to be that, because God's way—here is the third mark—is the way of utter fidelity. *"I will not cease in my efforts for their good."*

Even when God called the people to judgment, this consistently turned out to be His way of judgment: He decided in His people's favor against all enemies and even against their own willful, self-destructive sin. Did the people go into Babylonian exile? *Who is the author of this deed if not He who calls the generations from the beginning?* Even God's judgment is nothing more or less than an expression of His fidelity.

We need badly to hear this today. We tend to think, for one thing, when anything at all goes wrong in our lives, that we must have done something morally reprehensible to deserve it. We often feel strong but vague guilt when we face serious and enduring troubles. Perhaps because we justifiably blame ourselves for sinful actions day after day, we cannot imagine any wrong or suffering coming into our lives that does not come caused by or at least filtered through our own sinfulness.

We are more like God's people in ancient times that we would like to think. Hence, we need to accept this truth that helped them remain faithful to God: Nothing comes into our lives, not good and not bad, that does not fall under the power and the wisdom of the God who says to each of us as He said to Israel: *"You are precious in my eyes, and honored, and I love you."*

God is so faithful that He will not even let our own self-centeredness defeat His purpose. He will not let our own hardness repel Him. *"I will give them a different heart and a different way.... I will put respect for Me into their hearts, so that they turn from Me no more."*

We have another reason for needing to remember God's utter fidelity, a reason embedded in the lifeworld around us.

Humankind appears addicted to destructiveness. Just look around at the forty-odd wars now going on, not including the drug-wars in our own American cities. Look at the Black Forest denuded by acid rain, and the now barren hundreds of square miles around Chernobyl. Look at the human wastelands in slums and favellas. We are arrogant in ravishing the earth and corporately callous in ravishing the helpless among ourselves.

All of humanity should tremble to hear the threat Amos put into God's mouth: *The Lord Yahweh swears it by His own self: "I mean to abandon the city and all it contains."* There are times during the evening news when God seems to have carried out His threat and really has abandoned at least some of us.

Yet even Amos, as dyspeptic a prophet as any, recognized that he was feeling cantankerous because God's people were paying so little heed to God the Creator and Lord, and not because he was afraid that God would fail in fidelity. He knew, as we all do, that God's way *is faithful, without unfairness, uprightness itself and full of justice.*

Amos knew even more than that, and so do we. He knew that God tempers this uprightness and this justice, carrying on with us *like a shepherd feeding His flock, gathering lambs in His arms, holding them against His breast.* Over and over again, when God turns to restore, what He does goes far beyond the re-stocking of the store.

Here is the fourth mark of God's way: God keeps going beyond His original commitments and promises. Every breach on our part brings greater promises on God's, so that even Amos ends his liturgical lamentation with the expectation that *"The days are coming now—it is Yahweh who speaks—when harvest will follow directly after ploughing, the treading of grapes soon after sowing, and the mountains will run with new wine."*

We who do not belong to God's first people have benefited from His way of going beyond His original promises. When God sends the *joyful messenger to Zion,* He sends him not into the Temple where Israel alone would hear, but *up on a high mountain,* so that all the nations can hear (first reading). For the Lord intends to *summon a nation you never knew, so those unknown will come hurrying to you.* God's restoration means that a new people, gathered from every nation and people under heaven, will be able to say this: *"Come, let us go up to the mountain of Yahweh... that the God of Jacob may teach us His ways."*

God has chosen that the sins and stupidities even of those who did not belong to His first people will not lie outside of mercy. For God's way now lies open to all of humankind, and we can take as said to ourselves what was spoken to the original People of God: *"Console My people, console them,"* says your God. *"Speak to the heart of Jerusalem and call to her that her time of service is ended, that her sin is atoned for"* (first reading).

This raises the fifth mark of God's way, quite literally its sum and substance: God takes the initiative. God's are the first and the definitive steps in bringing together those who had parted company, in making atonement (at-one-ment). A California bumper-sticker proclaimed: "If God and you are far apart—who moved?" Another could as truly proclaim: "If you and God are together—who moved?"

All through the centuries, God's people had known God-for-us. God went out with their armies to defeat their enemies. God wiped away plagues and droughts. God sustained the people's faith and hope.

When the time had come for it, God consummated this saving work by becoming God-with-us. *Emmanuel* means more than surpassing hero and glorious victor. *Emmanuel* means God's transcendent Self in our own flesh.

This is how God makes all of humanity His own—by taking our nature to Himself. This is how God chose to give us a new heart, one on which He writes His law—by having a heart of His own.

Jesus puts it directly and simply: *"I am the way."*

This at-one-ment contains all the characteristics of God's way. God's way means that He lives utterly intimate with His own creatures even while remaining the Lord and mighty God. God's way means that we do not have to transform ourselves to find His way; it is in our flesh. No one of us has to be some other kind of person in order to love God; God's love now takes as its own way the way of human love. We do not have to make a new heart and a new person of ourselves in order to stand before His face and serve Him; He has chosen to come into our old heart, to fill our old heart with His justice, mercy, and love. For *through the blood of Jesus,* God has opened for us in His own Self *a new way, a living opening,* as the author of Hebrews put it. Here is what Paul meant when he exclaimed, *"For me to live is Christ!"* Because God has so chosen, every single one of us can make that same claim. *To live is Christ.*

By now, the conclusion of all this has become fairly plain: Finding God's way means first of all searching our own heart and flesh. We will find buried deep there tremendous thirsts and desires—to give life and to save, to live faithful and loyal and to restore what has decayed. Above all, to live at one with all whom we know.

These thirsts and desires are now filled with God's own thirsts and desires; they are a share in God's own. Indeed, they have been all along, even while we were unaware of it.

For this one thing is transcendently true of God's way: He begins. He takes the initiative always. He creates momently.

Prepare a way for the Lord? We start by saying thanks for all that has been and is. And we let that thanksgiving become an openness to all that is to come, as our God takes His own gracious way.

What kind of God have we who chooses rainbows as the divine symbol?

Can we really trust that God will raise in us desires for Himself above all, quelling all empty yearnings, and so prepare a way in us? What are those desires?

In the end, no one can know how God chooses to deal with us who does not already grasp that God always begins all that lives.

Prayer

When we think to prepare a way for You,
Lord God, Lamb of God,
we act as if we believe
You are reluctant to come.

For we try to make ourselves so holy
that You will have to come and love us.

We try to make ourselves so just
that in justice You will have to come and live with us.

We confess that we discourage ourselves
for not doing what we cannot do;
we blame ourselves
for failing to do what we need not do.

Teach us, Master,
that we need not encourage You to come.

We need not,
for Your way is to set our first,
to summon light where the dark prevailed,
to sustain the life You have created.

Your way is to come Yourself to us in our way,
to search for the lost sheep,
to run out and meet the returning runaway,
to go out and contend gently with the elder son.

Come, we hear You saying, Lord,
come away from the chaos which I have defeated.
Come into celebration.
Lord, however it looks, we mean to come.   Amen.

6. Remembered by God

I am sure of this much: He who has begun the good work in you will carry it through to completion.

Time and again, the people of Israel were subjugated or exiled. Time and again, they forgot God the Lord, worshiped other gods, and ended in *mourning and misery.* In their relationship with God, these behaviors fell into patterns, and the patterns gave shape to their history. The people listened to this history when—time and again—prophets appeared to remind them of who they were and to call them to repentance.

For Israel could truly repent only to the extent that the people understood who they were. They could really allow God to change their hearts only when they recalled how differently they had gotten along with their God in the past from the way they were getting along with their God in the present. Through the patterns of their past, they came to understand themselves and their God. In that understanding, they were able to hear what God wanted of them and hoped for them in the present.

That is why Moses, Isaiah, and John the Baptist reminded them of the past. As long as they remembered, they could believe in the present that *God leads Israel in joy by the light of His glory, with His mercy and justice for company* (first reading).

What was and continues true of Israel is true of each of us who are now God's people. That is the significance of what Paul said to the Philippians: *"I am sure of this much, that He who has begun the good work in you will carry it through to completion, right up to the day of Christ Jesus"* (second reading).

We have lived that faith since our baptism. We have developed habits and virtues within it, faced within it our crises, and enjoyed within it our successes. Within that faith, too, we have suffered from our own limitations, committed our own sins, and repented. As God stayed with His people Israel, so God has stayed with each of us, sustaining in us the impulse to grow *in understanding and wealth of experience*.

Well now, that's very pretty but it raises a problem. The problem is that God may stay with us, but we do not stay with God. At least, we do not have the experience of staying with God. For here is the reality all too common among us: We remember God cherishing us momently a little more often than we remember the Book of the Prophet Baruch, but not a lot more. Almost every one of us remembers Baruch's lovely book once a year—unless we miss the one Sunday Mass that takes a passagej from it. Well, how often do most of us sit in quiet, purring in the deep joy of God's caring attention to us?

The truth about many adult disciples is a little desolate: We do not remember that we live in God's presence. In fact, we do not find it easy to actively believe that God relates to each one of us steadily, courteously, and patiently.

This oblivion, this forgetfulness of God, is hardly new among humankind. People never have found it easy to remember God busy in their lives, and the reasons are enough to persuade us to join them in their oblivion, if we are not already there.

To begin with, it is a very inconvenient belief. It requires of us that we return God's steady, courteous, and patient attention. To speak very candidly, most of us do not give steady, courteous, and patient attention even to ourselves, whom we feel most inclined so to favor. A rare spouse gives it to the beloved other, who may or may not return it. We find giving that kind of attention to anyone extravagantly difficult, and particularly to God.

In fact, the desolate reality goes even deeper. Many otherwise sensible people today cannot believe that God cares about the ordinary things in their daily lives. They seem to believe that rain, stock markets, epidemic infections, the mechanics of the automobile, and perhaps word processors, lie outside of God's authority. Some few professors of theology—some very, very few, every one of whom really ought to know better—have asked us to wonder whether revelation contains that belief in God's special, personal providence. They should be aware that they are emptying of their certain meaning many things said by Jesus Christ *"Are you not worth many sparrows?"* and they are flouting many things written by the authors of scripture and by the great Fathers of the Church.

Many other mature disciples have no speculative problems, but they are absorbed by the psychological working of their own minds, or engrossed in getting and enjoying consumer goods, so that their practical faith does not include a caring God. Certainly they believe in God, but they believe God preoccupied somewhere else with unimaginably massive concerns. Some good Christians have their faith stunned by massive evils like the war in the Middle East or the plague of drug abuse spread around our nation. Where is God when your cousin is an addict? For many of the highly trained, too, a scientific God has practically disappeared into "transcendence." For them, God has gotten so far removed from our daily lives that He makes the "Watchmaker God" of the Enlightenment seem like an English nanny. Probably every serious disciple knows Christians who have been (in the strict sense of the word) scandalized in one or other of these ways.

Yet our faith is clear: God deals individually with each ofjus, individually calling our immortal life out of the unformed possibilities of matter and mind. The Eucharist means at least that, surely.

So did the way the God of Jesus Christ dealt differently with those whose lives touched His Son's. John the Baptist, whose burst into prophecy we read in the Gospel, had been consecrated as an infant to live a godly life in the scorching desert, eating ghastly things. Isaiah before him, whose 700-year-old oracle John cited, had been formed from his mother's womb to marry and live a godly life at home in the wicked city, eating his wife's cooking.

Peter, though one of those called to followed Jesus from the start, had to live with the realization that he was flaccid enough to deny to a pushy little girl that he knew Jesus. Coming later, Paul's antecedents as Jew and Roman citizen shaped him to courage, and he risked death many times for Christ's sake.

Each human life touched by God the Lord takes a special shape and pattern as God accomplishes what He hopes for: Martha and Mary, Zacchaeus and the rich young man, Nathaniel without guile who did not become an apostle and Thomas full of doubt who did. Each of our lives takes shape under pressures and invitations that fall within God's dominion: racial, familial, economic, educational, regional, professional. We are foolish not to grasp that it is surely not irrelevant to God's love for us and our love for God that we be Chicano or Polish, wellmarried or passably, cheerfully confused or neurotically plagued, affluent or on welfare, tall or short, long-lived or decrepit at twenty-eight. For God the Lord owns responsibility for any such patterns just the way a friend or lover wants shared responsibility for everything that touches the course of a friendship or of a love.

That is what Paul referred to when he talked about *that rich harvest of justice which Jesus Christ is ripening in you.* We truly live with His life, and bear the fruit He intended. The Father is the vine-dresser, who had already decided what kind of grape to plant and where to plant it and how much water to bring it in irrigation. The Father knows what to do with the blood of the grape and when to come for the harvest.

In our own freedom, of course, we are responsible for the patterns of our lives. But we are mistaken to try to take responsibility for matters over which we have no control. That demand for responsibility will lead only to discouragement and to disbelief.

Then, too, we tend to overestimate the scope of our freedom, perhaps in an unspoken demand to have total control over who we are and over what comes into our lives. We tend to think that we are equally free in all of our choices and actions, which is quite manifestly not the case. We need to recognize that our freedom is truly and densely limited by our own Godgiven limitations, by the limits that our lifeworld places on us, and even by others' freedoms and willfulnesses. We are made less free by the pressures of an unkind boss and more free by the invitations of a beloved spouse.

All of those limitations, we can perceive as crushing and dehumanizing burdens, the assessment encouraged by our lifeworld. Our contemporaries demand a kind and a degree of freedom that, limited creatures in time and place that we are, we cannot actually have. So they live tied up in knots by advertising and fashion and fad, and slavishly follow whatever habits they happen to form.

For ourselves, we can if we choose perceive every limitation imposed upon us as the wish of God our Lord, just another part of the way God our Lord remains mindful of us. We are free to recognize fashion and fad as helpful, usually, and fine; but skin-deep and of no ultimate importance whatsoever. We are free to live without grieving over foolish mistakes and embarrassing compulsions, free indeed to live content to be so limited. God is much bigger than any of these, and God stands, as Paul said, *on our side*. So *who can be against us* and have any final effect?

Every year, we hear the prophets speaking out and the church teaching how God has begun this work in us and will carry it through. They call us to repentance and to a change of heart. To repent for what? In what particular are we to change our heart? Each of us will know; for the patterns in our past lives tell us how God has chosen to deal with us, whether we willingly served or willfully rebelled.

Each of us can come to experience the way God has steadily, courteously, and patiently stayed with us all through our years. When we accept this experience from the Spirit, we will know where we need repentance and a change of heart, and perhaps where we are summoned to penitence. But like the whole People of Israel, we will not be able to know how God leads us in the present unless we acknowledge the patterns in our lifelong relationship with the Lord. And we will repent of nothing, and embrace no growth in spirit, unless we commit ourselves to the hope that *He who began the good work in us will carry it through to completion.*

The first question has to be whether we truly believe that our whole life can rightly be called *God's good work.*

We recognize that we live through passages and phases and stages, which social scientists have named. We might wonder whether we can name patterns and passages of our growth in Christ.

In the last analysis, we might harm someone by acting unjustly, but we never hurt anyone the way we hurt those who love us when we park them on the periphery of our life. Each of us needs to reflect whether we have made that the pattern of our life with God. Have we parked God on the periphery?

Prayer

Almighty and ever-watchful God,
though the lilies of the fields do not spin
and the birds of the air do not make crops,
yet they are vested in splendor
and find all the nutrients they need.

For You who give them life
bring them to flower and to song,
and then shape their lives to completion in seed.

Yet we who are more precious to You than all of these
and must justly rely on Your care,
have fought Your mastery.

We have tried with all our cunning
to control every pattern in our own life,
to force success,

to win approval,
to have all the things we think we want,
to select each energy and ability that drives us.

We confess to You now,
Lord God, heavenly King,
You are our maker, and not we ourselves.

We confess that all the patterns that have shaped our life
fall now and always have fallen under Your mastery,
and our sins could never unmake You.

For You are God
and You steadily, patiently, courteously,
raise the sun on our mornings
and guard us while we sleep
and give us those whom we love and who love us.

We come before You, holy God, to confess
that our entire life and our whole self
is a good work
which we beg You
to carry through to completion.

Amen.

7. A Long Winter's Wait

"Happy is the man who does not lose faith in Me."

John the Baptizer lies in prison. From all around, his disciples bring him stories about Jesus' activities. John takes it all in and then at some juncture sends his disciples to ask Jesus a question: *"Are You the One who is to come, or have we got to wait for someone else?"*

Why would John send disciples to ask that?

When he baptized Jesus on the banks of the Jordan, John had seemed certain enough who Jesus was. He had taken a definite stand about his own relationship to Jesus, proclaiming himself the one of whom Isaiah had prophesied: *"A voice that cries in the wilderness, 'Make a straight way for the Lord.'"* John had recognized his Lord and had said quietly to two of his disciples that Jesus was indeed *the Lamb of God.* He had said loudly to anyone who would listen, long before Herod had thrown him into prison: *"Yes, I have seen and I am the witness that He is the Chosen One of God."*

John gave very clear evidence of feeling certain that he knew who and what Jesus was, according to the record we have. They why did he ask from prison, *"Are You the One?"*

Each of three plausible explanations opens up some truths not only about John but, perhaps even more, about Jesus the Christ and about ourselves.

First of all, there is the possibility that John did not need to know for himself and did not ask for himself. He needed his disciples to know and sent them to ask for themselves. After all, John recognized his disciples for what they were—zealots who felt a keen loyalty to their leader. He knew that he would have to work actively to shift their allegiance to the One whom he recognized as Master of them all. He may well have felt that he did not have much time for that, anticipating that he would die in prison. So he got a start by sending them to query Jesus.

We know for sure that John had all along been eager to help his people shift their loyalty to Jesus. He had said to them publicly, *"He must grow greater; I must grow smaller."*

If this is the explanation why John sent his disciples to Jesus, it holds an important lesson for those of us who are now charged with bringing others to our Master. For while he must already have told them that they were to follow Jesus, and given them solid scriptural arguments to help them, John knew that every good argument for knowing and loving Jesus Christ is incarnate. He was himself such an argument—and he acted out his own devotion to Jesus precisely by sending his disciples to Jesus. If in our own lives we are not ourselves good arguments for the truth of Jesus' Good News, then what we say will convince no one. Pope Paul VI once said that postmodern men and women are not looking for teachers, but for witnesses; and if people today listen approvingly to anyone, that is because the speaker embodies what he or she proclaims. In just that way, we are God's evidence that the Christ has already come, and that God has *indeed made all things new.*

If that honor seems just too good to be true, keep in mind how Jesus compared John the Baptizer to any one of us: *"I tell you solemnly, of all the children born of women, one greater than John the Baptist has never been seen; yet the least in the kingdom of heaven is greater than he is."* Could it be that we have underestimated the dignity of those who receive the Body and Blood into themselves? Have we treated too lightly the status—and the responsibilities—of those who can ask *and it will be given to them?*

John gave no sign of hesitating to ask what he wanted, and he has impressed most commentators as having posed an honest question and expected a straightforward answer. So there is a second feasible explanation why John sent from prison to Jesus.

John had predicted at the Jordan that Jesus the Messiah had come to do some rather dramatic things. Locked in prison, however, John heard no stories of Jesus doing those things that he had predicted. So he needed reassurance. Was Jesus indeed the Messiah? As it is recorded in his preaching, John's image of the Messiah included superhuman endowments. He saw *the axe laid to the roots of the trees* that were not bringing forth good fruit. He saw Jesus sweeping away any who opposed Him. John cited Isaiah and Jeremiah: *"He will clear His threshing-floor and gather His wheat into the barn; but the chaff He will burn in a fire that will never go out."*

Furthermore, John returned out of the desert to a nation agog with expectation. The people were caught up in one of their periodic paroxysms, looking for a grand, universal kingdom. They heard the voice of Yahweh like thunder in Spring: *"I am going to gather all the nations."* They half-feared and half-hoped that they would be astounded—today? tonight?—by the cataclysmic events of the Day of the Lord. They could almost feel in the earth under their feet the arrival of Isaiah's promise: *"Let the wilderness and the dry lands exult!"*

In other words, the people felt that when the Messiah came to bring the Kingdom, they would have no doubt whether He and the Kingdom had arrived.

Well, John might have wondered, had He? Who could believe that this awesome Messiah was embodied in John's cousin, enjoying wedding-feasts, fondling children, traipsing around the Galilee with a motley entourage, cooling fevered faces with His touch, one more man among the sweaty crowd? The One-to-Come was to gather armies to fervid battle, not just a small group of close friends to talk with warmly. Had Jesus swung into action with great power? Had He begun to look like a triumphant king? Could He even be thought a likely candidate to get to be such a great king some day?

So John sat in jail remembering the promises and pondering what he himself had prophesied. His head swarmed with dramatic images of the endtime. Perhaps he really did send his disciples out to request reassurance from his Friend.

We should be able to resonate with that need for reassurance. We sit, if not in jail, at least through long times in the prison of not knowing where our life is going, or our lifeworld. We surely need to query the Christ who promised to remain with us, whether He remains content at the way things are going. We might even feel the need to remind Christ of the way things are going. Like Teresa of Avila: As she walked on an apostolic journey once, she fell into a mudhole, and perhaps only partially in humor told God it was no wonder He had so few friends—look how He treats them. If our faith has reached the strength of simplicity, we often need to ask Him to come quickly, to get moving, to let us feel His help.

We have moved from the second to the third possible explanation why John might have sent to Jesus. For possibly, just as we sometimes urgently desire that God would get moving and do something, John urgently desired that the Messiah would get moving in His work.

John did indeed sit in jail remembering the vivid prophecies and pondering the course of his Cousin's life. Jesus had begun in obscurity and had tested His calling in the desert, perhaps with John himself. He had begun public life quietly, knee-deep in Jordan. Now, John might have thought, now was the time to start fulfilling those prophecies.

The idea might seem fanciful, but it does explain Jesus' answer. He did not answer yes or no to John's direct question whether He were the One to come. What He really did was tell John what kind of Messiah He felt Himself to be. He reminded him of some other prophecies about the coming of the Messiah, milder ones that did not include cataclysm. He said in effect that the images of royal splendor and cosmic uproar were just that—images. The reality of the dawning Reign of God was in His work of teaching and of healing. *The eyes of the blind shall be opened, the ears of the deaf unsealed* (Gospel).

If He seemed to neglect the prophecies that the Messiah would move in great power, He was actually preparing to bring every one of them to fulfillment. John had called Jesus *the Lamb of God,* aware of the self-sacrifice that symbolized. John surely knew that Jesus was calling Himself *the Son of Man,* and he would have understood what Jesus alluded to by the title Isaiah cherished. He was going to sacrifice Himself for the people's sins, and *in being lifted up* would show the great power of God.

This Messiah fulfilled all of the prophecies of victory and triumph, but in His own way and not in the world's way. His victory does not look at all like the victories of great generals and kings and rulers. In fact, it hardly looks like a victory at all except to a very small, chosen few. The reason is simple: His victory is not like the victories that the world exalts. Who in the world would recognize a victory in which no one was defeated?

Jesus' victory is more like the seed's victory which has to die in order to replicate its own life. His victory is one for which we have to wait as a farmer patiently waits for the precious fruit of the ground (second reading).

We might recognize that in this waiting we are a little like John the Baptist. We want everyone to come to Christ, too. We want reassurance that Christ remains the One-to-Come, for us. We need Him to hurry up and get the Reign established everywhere, forever.

Like the Baptist, we have to wait. We wait for that gentle, life-giving victory, not only abroad in all the world, but also deep within our own lives and our own selves. Our wait surely seems long. The world's wait— while so many starve and go ignorant and die as children and quail before life—sometimes seems unending, a very long winter's wait in dark and cold.

And blessed are they who do not lose faith in Him.

Now would be a good time to ask ourselves bluntly what we expect Jesus Christ to do.

We could, again, wonder whether we say in our lives, "You are indeed the One," or whether we are waiting for someone else.

What are we to make of this: That each of us who belong to the Kingdom, through baptism and God's love, are to believe ourselves greater than as great a man as was ever born of woman before the Kingdom came?

Prayer

Lord Jesus Christ,
we are astounded that even
the little ones in the Kingdom
can be compared to John the Baptist,
Your good and faithful friend.

We do not see it, Lord,
we do not see the splendor of Your work in us.

We fear that if we did see it,
we would get proud and full of self
and wreck it.

Yet this we know:
We hold You high.
We praise You, we worship You, we glorify You.
And that is Your work in us,
for we would not know to do it
on our own.

We hold to this,
we hold to You,
and then we can wait
through the world's long winter
in deep content.

Amen.

8. What God Expects

Be happy at all times.

Starting with the first of all the letters he wrote, the first one to the Thessalonians, Paul the Apostle tried to describe how Christians behave. He did not have much tradition to go on; he wrote his first letter a spare twenty years after Jesus Christ had ascended to the Father.

Still, he and all of the early leaders were able to judge certain ways of behaving from the very start. For instance, Paul declared to the members of just about every church he wrote to, *Attend your own business and earn your living.* He was not borrowing a moral dictum from his stoical contemporary Seneca; he was correcting Christians who expected the Last Day to come and solve all their problems.

That situation seemed clear enough, but others did not. Paul had to struggle in his own mind and then had to battle Peter and James over the question whether pagan converts had to be circumcised and follow the whole Law.

A man trained in religion, Paul had certain basic insights into the way Christian behavior expresses the life of Christ in us. He was always applying and developing those basic insights, no matter what particular behavior he addressed. His thumbnail sketches of Christian life, as a consequence, have a certain consistency and coherence.

However, Paul kept keenly aware of events and circumstances, and he was always applying his basic insights in the concrete. As a consequence of that, his descriptions of Christian include some items that barely pertain to us at all. When he wrote to the Thessalonians, for instance, he had to deal with their anxiety over the parousia (they thought it was coming momentarily) and he had to encourage them in the very physical persecutions they were suffering from their countrymen. Were he writing today, he would have to chide Christians for thinking too little of the last things, and find a way to keep us from feeling bad that we don't even have much anti-Catholicism or anti-Christian sentiment to brave any more, let alone any true persecution.

One consequence of all this is some confusion over which of Paul's mandates pertain to our own lives. Some plainly do, such as this one: *Be at peace among yourselves* (second reading). In this case, even Paul's development of the mandate bears directly on our lives at the end of the twentieth century. For he went on to specify a number of ways of dealing with one another that suggest a very active community life: *Warn the idlers, give courage to those who are apprehensive, care for the weak, and be patient with everyone.* Paul meant *everyone,* including those who wrong us, for he added that no one should *try to take revenge.* This mandate plainly addresses our life experience in an age of anxiety and shifting human relations, as do very many others. We need to hear as much as the Colossians did, to cite one more instance, that we, *of all people, must give all these things up: getting angry, being bad-tempered, spitefulness, abusive language and dirty talk; and never tell each other lies.*

On the other hand, some of Paul's and the other inspired writers' mandates plainly do not address anything in our real lives. Probably, for example, very few of us have to worry that we will cause anyone scruples by eating *food that was offered in sacrifice,* a thing the Corinthians had to guard against. Again, since circumcision is now a medical matter, we do not have to *watch out for the cutters,* who were trying to persuade the Galatians and the Philippians to accept circumcision as a sign of submission to the whole Law. Some scriptural mandates even make us wince— *Slaves, be obedient to the men who are called your masters in this world*

—and force us to ponder a long time on our beliefs and our principles of behavior.

A third group of mandates in scripture also bring us up short. Do they or do they not apply to us? They sound important, but do not exactly ring out with relevancy. A prime example (to arrive finally at the topic of these reflections) would be this odd command: *Be happy at all times.* Can we who feel so keenly our psychological baggage—and who daily gaze on local disasters all around the global village—can we take *Be happy at all times* seriously as a principle of mature life in Christ? How can anyone mandate happiness to begin with? Isn't this really an exhortation for beginners? Paul, after all, was addressing disciples who were beginners in every conceivable way.

Even if he were not, the mandate *Be happy* sounds to our super-psychologized ears like a platitude belched up by an undercertified swami. Or like one of the jewels that Americans pay hundreds of dollars to collect during a weekend of sensitivity training. Would anyone say *Be happy at all times* to the Christian guards at Ossining or Leavenworth? That seems naive. Will anyone try *Be happy* on parents whose children have quit churchgoing and started doing drugs? That verges on the sardonic. Could it be that people who have transmuted moral earnestness nearly into a misery are right about *taking up the Cross?*

Well, Paul knew the Cross: labor, suffering, and absurdity. He was writing this letter and its mandate from Corinth, which in his day was the capital of the absurd. As a matter of fact, he had arrived at Corinth from Thessolonika after a faintly absurd experience there. He had been forced to slip out of that little city in the middle of the night because his enemies *had the whole city in an uproar* and were trying to pin the ruction on Paul. Actually, the further back into his situation he looked, the more absurd it all seemed. He came to Corinth, capital of the absurd, because he had been driven out of Thessolonika, and he had gone to Thessolonika in the first place because he had been flogged out of Philippi.

Paul's whole life proceeded through conflicts and sufferings pretty much on that same order, so he was hardly naive. He could be sardonic, as he was when he expressed the hope, concerning those among the Galatians who were accepting circumcision, *that the knife slip.*

In the midst of all that, when he wrote *Be happy at all times*, he was stating a spiritual principle that he had proven out in his own life.

We need to hold on to that point: This principle of life in Christ has been validated by a great deal of experience. In nothing are the mystics and the theologians and the great doctors of the church as unanimous as in this, that living a faithful life in Christ means great happiness. An ancient ritual prayer exemplifies this. It was spoken to women or men who had just pronounced perpetual vows as they accepted the vow cross that they would hold in their hands in the grave: "May he to whom your life is offered give you through the cross, joy and fortitude in perseverance." Centuries of experience of austere monastic life taught the church to expect, under the shadow of the Cross and in the middle of fortitude and endurance, joy.

The authorities concur also, however, that only men and women who see their life marked by God's initiatives from the start can live *happy at all times.* Our joy flows precisely from the fact that God begins us and our life and everything in our world.

The Mother of Jesus showed plainly that her joy worked that way. The angel told Mary to *"Rejoice, so highly favored."* And Mary answered from her heart: *"My soul proclaims the greatness of the Lord; my spirit exults..."* She could say that because of what was already established in her spirit, the operative belief that *"He who is mighty has done great things for me."* In this woman's life—not because she was a woman and not because she was a little girl, but because she was a wise human being—God's initiatives came first.

Mary was citing Isaiah (first reading), who had added these words from the mouth of the Lord: *"You shall see my servants rejoice... You shall hear my servants sing for joy of heart."* Isaiah intended to make the point that it is God's choice that we should live joyfully. This is important, because Isaiah was addressing an inveterate human worry that our desire for happiness itself affronts the gods. Much of humankind has felt that any happiness or joy in their lives had been stolen from the gods, and angered them. Isaiah taught a very different doctrine.

The desire to live happy itself rises first of all from God's infinite happiness and the inexhaustible divine desiring for bliss. The One who makes us, makes us in the divine image and as a matter of course imbues us with this same desiring. If the Creator puts the desire in us for joy, then the Creator intends that we shall have joy. That, as the Christmas story has come down to us, is one of the first things said about God's definitive entry into human life and affairs. Whatever the literary husk around the angels' song to the shepherds, the kernel of the message was this: *"I bring you news of great joy."* The Good News is very, very good news.

Later on, when Jesus began to announce the Good News, He marked it with happiness. We should never forget that just as He moved into public life and before He had done any works of power in public, He took the disciples He had gathered to a wedding party at Cana. That's the first thing: He took them to a party. And then an even more significant thing: When the party was coming to an unplanned end because of lack of supplies, He moved up what He had thought an appropriate time for works of power and gave them more wine. More *of the best wine.* We need to remember that *this was the first of the signs given by Jesus,* the Master whose mind we are to put on and whose behavior stands as a model for our own. Anybody who can't read this message of joy must be a congenital grouch.

Think, too, of His parables. If we can set aside for just one moment the moral weight they lay on us, we find that they are full of happy people. The widow who found her lost drachma was delighted. The man who happened on a treasure in the field gleefully bartered away everything to get that field. The good shepherd felt deep joy when he found the lost sheep. (There is joy in heaven when a sinner leaves sin.) A great king gave a banquet and when some of those invited turned out to be dunces, he filled his hall with riffraff so his banquet could be a smashing success. (The banquet in the Kingdom will be such a smashing success.) The father of the prodigal insisted to his dullard elder son that, *"It is only right that we should celebrate and rejoice."* (That father, Jesus tried to make us understand, is only a vague mock-up of the passionately, joyfully merciful heavenly Father.)

Jesus did not limit happiness to His stories. He filled with joy those who came near Him. *All the people,* when they were left untroubled by rulers and lawyers to react spontaneously, *all the people were overjoyed at the wonders He worked.* Little Zacchaeus *welcomed Him joyfully.* The seventy-two disciples were tickled to have worked some wonders of their own. When Jesus rode a donkey into Jerusalem, *the disciples began joyfully to praise God at the top of their voices.* And, to close the list with the very last item of all, when Jesus came back from the dead to console His friends, *their joy was so great that they could not believe it.*

Indeed they could not, and their struggle with joy began a centuries-long struggle to accept the joy that is the Christians' right even in this gritty world. Why in the world would we struggle with—or better, against—joy in our lives?

The first of our tactics to turn joyful living into a struggle emerges from our general strategy to make ourselves happy. That is to say, we try to make ourselves happy instead of trusting God to make us happy. How do we do this? We try to dictate what possessions, status, jobs, will make us happy, and we refuse to let our experience teach us otherwise. A lot of miserable people with hefty bank accounts persist in believing that a few more thousand will let them break through into total happiness. Some people follow an advancement in their careers right out of a situation in which they and their families have plainly found everything they need, into a situation that truly threatens desperate stresses on their marriages and perhaps disastrous teen-ages for their children. They are trying to dictate to the Lord what will make them happy. And they are surely disappointed.

We insist on determining completely on our own which among all our gifts and abilities are the ones that we will follow out to become completely happy. So today we are faced with the absurdity of a person whose gifts add up to marriage and child-rearing, demanding happiness from a single life and a business career. We find disciples with tremendous manual dexterity and moderate intellectual endowments rejecting any kind of manual labor and demanding happiness from a career in counseling. And we face a lot of very faithful and very intelligent Christians who demand that their third-grade grasp of the truths of the faith be sufficient for their interior joy, even though they may have graduate degrees.

This exigent way of life differs from the way of finding out what desires, possessions, jobs, abilities, opportunities, will make us happy. When we try things and wait to find out what makes us happy, we are trying to discover God's hopes for us. For the way of joy is the way of the dialogue between the creature and the Creator; it is never a one-way street. So when we decide beforehand what will make us happy and then demand that our decision be the correct one, we are usurping God's role.

This is a complicated matter, but keep in mind that when we say "life is a gift" we are not speaking about an abstraction, but about the concrete, everyday reality that is this and that real life. God gives that concrete gift of life, with all its concrete particulars. Well, the receiver of a gift does not demand the gift. The receiver of a gift does not expect to determine what the gift will be. Neither do we decide beforehand, without waiting to learn God's hopes, what will make us happy. Any disciples who are not aware of sinning in their lives but who nonetheless find life not a joy but a struggle might consider whether this is the strategy they are following.

The second of our strategies to turn joy into struggle involves our sin and our sinful beliefs. If we are not happy, we can expect to find a definite, finite reason in our own lives, not in our lifeworld. We might find an habitual sin that we cling to, like persons who bitterly resent their alcoholic parents and refuse to forgive them. We might realize that we have cast the Creator in a role repugnant to God's true Self, or that we cling to some strange beliefs, like the one expressed in a ditty on a "holy card": "Jesus, My Lord, I have crucified Thee/Now it is Thy turn, crucify me." Of course, that prayer could express a desire to identify with the Lord, who embraced *death, and death on a cross.* But any disciple who believes that Jesus Christ could treat one whom He loves the way the one whom He loves has treated Him has bought a belief that will lead to life as a struggle and not to life as a joy.

We really have no reason to doubt, in the last analysis, whether Paul meant this mandate of happiness for all of us. If we continue to find the mandate a bit odd, we need to remember that Paul did not derive it either from his own theological principles or from his own experience. He simply reported what Jesus Christ had said and had done.

Paul repeated this mandate in various forms and in various contexts in his letters. In the letter to the Thessalonians, he linked it with two other mandates: *Be happy at all times. Pray constantly. And for all things, give thanks to God.*

Connected this way, *be happy* does not seem such an odd command, even if we have to carry it out differently from the other two. In any case, it is what we are called to. As Paul concludes about all three mandates, *"this is what God expects you to do in Christ Jesus."*

Can we trust that our desire to live happy itself comes out of God's infinite desire for bliss?

Any mature follower of Jesus Christ recognizes the differences between pleasure and happiness.

What thing, what activity, what job, what relationship, could make it worth our while to give up our Christian birthright of living happy at all times

---

Prayer

Spirit of the Living God,
deep in the holy reaches of eternity
You live in utter bliss
in a joy that blinds our little happiness
the way the light of the sun overwhelms a match's flame.

How gracious You are to share with us
the happiness of the Father and the Son,

and Your own joy in their creating
and re-creating love.

How gracious to draw up from our selves
an unslakeable thirst for joy,
and then to give us Your own Wisdom
so that we can discern
among the teeming good things of God's earth
what will outlast pleasure
and grow into happiness.

Holy and mighty Spirit,
lift us at every moment, at all times,
out of nothingness and the chaos of evil
into the happiness
You are shaping in us to last forever and ever. Amen.

9. Again: Rejoice

Rejoice in the Lord always!

When we tell anyone, "Take it easy," we tell them something everyone understands, whether a boss in a fit of pique or an acrobat at the peak of fitness. "Take it easy," we understand, and "Hang in there," and "Right on."

"Rejoice" is something else. Anyone who says that is quoting Scripture or Shakespeare. We just might understand "Rejoice" at a wedding with six bridesmaids, or at a midnight Mass. But we would feel bemused by "Rejoice" coming from a receptionist or from our tax accountant.

If the fact that we do not get much of a message when told to rejoice were due just to fashion in language, it would not be bad at all. Words come and words go. But there's more to the fact that we listen and do not hear, and that is bad. For Paul said that the disciples of Christ are to *rejoice always,* and he was saying no more than the Master said. Jesus told His disciples that He would teach them all He knew *"so that my joy may be yours and your joy may be complete."* Surely a complete joy would fill all days and not be darkened by anything that came along. *Rejoice always.*

The mandate must be feasible, for God does not order impossible things. Paradoxically, disciples of Christ who are serious do in fact live joyful lives. On a larger scale, if any quality besides exuberance marks the

57

North American church, it is joyfulness. Grouches on the left and on the right feel left out precisely because the body of the church lives so joyfully. We can even analyze our joyfulness without fear of losing it the way you lose brandy when you set it on fire to pour over fruit. For in a very real way, *Rejoice always* turns out to be a gift given just as much as a mandate to be fulfilled.

Any analysis would have to start by setting aside the lives of those who recklessly violate their own consciences. Men and women who go from pride to greed to lust to anger, playing hopscotch among the capital sins, will take a lot of pleasure and perhaps sometimes feel hilarity. They will not know joy. In fact, to state an important law of the spiritual life, God will work in them to make them feel unhappy and joyless so they will change their sinful ways.

Serious disciples, men and women who really try to follow their consciences even though they fail all the time, find God dealing differently with themselves. God gives them joy and God gives them courage. We have the testimony of a saint who knew something about this: St. John Chrysostom said in one of his sermons that we have no grounds "to grieve unaccountable sins, be they over and over." Maybe that he knew what addiction is.

In any case, serious disciples who live joyful lives fulfill one precondition and have four outstanding qualities.

The precondition: We take full responsibility for our own lives, as any truly mature adult must. How? We acknowledge candidly that everything we have gone through has been a dialogue between the self and God. We see clearly that the man and woman who are our parents were given that grace by God the Creator. We see clearly that our talents and intelligence, our education and rearing have shaped us in concrete ways and put concrete limits on us. Those concrete ways and limits, we consider coming directly from the hand of God our Creator and Lord.

But at the same time, we recognize that our free choices within those limits shaped us more deeply than anything else. We have done wrong, perhaps truly grievous wrong, perhaps over a long time. Or, we have accepted grace, perhaps unusually great grace, toward holiness of life. Or, we have gotten into and out of sinful ways, and still have hard things to deal with in our habits and behaviors.

Well, if we live in deep and abiding happiness, then we really have taken responsibility for all of it. We accept it as our own, as a long dialogue with God our Creator.

Then—to name the first of the four qualities of a joy-filled life—we accept our life history and our self as belonging to God. Not that we feel the way slaves feel, who belong as chattels to another human person. Very much the contrary; as Paul told the Romans, *the spirit you received is not the spirit of slaves bringing fear into your lives again.* To know that we belong to God means to know a tremendous freedom, *the freedom of the children of God,* the freedom of those who live in a benevolent country full of friendly forces.

Our faith wells up within us to proclaim through the joy of our lives what each of the readings for this Sunday proclaims: *The King of Israel, the Lord, is in your midst,* as Zephaniah put it. And Paul, *The Lord is near.*

If our faith does not well up far enough, we tend to hold God at arm's length. We then take the *near* in the odd sense that God is at some distance. We might even believe not that the Lord has come, but that the Lord is about to come, for Paul probably alludes to the parousia in his statement. However, Paul certainly reasserts what he always insists upon, whether the parousia comes this afternoon or centuries from now: Christ is intimately present in all of us. *Life for me, of course, is Christ,* he wrote to the Philippians; and to the Romans, *the present given by God is eternal life in Christ Jesus our Lord.*

Every Christian who lives joyful has this sense, that Jesus Christ has been and is now aware of me, the way I am—perplexed, confused, loving, holy, sinning, selfless, however I am right now—and steadily loves me into life. Not that every joyful Christian thinks about that at every moment; we live steadily convinced of it and that conviction drives our daily lives.

Along with the conviction that Christ dwells in us comes a second quality. Joyful Christians readily feel a harmony between what comes into their life and God's creative love.

This is hope, the great antidote to anxiety. In fact, feeling a harmony between what actually happens and God's creative love helps us to *dismiss all anxiety from our minds.* This feeling of harmony comes as a gift from the God of harmony, and allows us to trust what happens to us even when we are painfully pressed by inequities and inanities. We find Christ modeling this for us, who stood with sinners for baptism by John and was hanged on His cross in a row of thieves. He always did the next good thing, and trusted in the Father.

A third quality, obviously closely connected with the second, stands out as crucial in our time. Joyful Christians live in the serene conviction that human existence has meaning. We come up against blank walls just as often as our unbelieving friends come up against them. "Why is this happening to me?" "How could God let that happen to such a good person?" We have the gift of incorporating these blank walls into the landscape of our interior life without letting them transmute it into a surrealist nightmare.

This sense that life has meaning does not flow from a philosophical commitment to a rational order, as it does in some people's courageous lives. In us, it starts as a conviction, and it remains a dynamic conviction right in the face of the Cross, the mere shadow of which pressures rational order to smithereens. This conviction, no one earns; it is a gift to feel meaning in "what I have done and what I have failed to do," in what has been visited upon me by others both responsibly and irresponsibly, or pressed upon me by my lifeworld.

Paul found meaning even in the absurdities he met with at Antioch in Pisidia, where jealous religious leaders stirred up women of the upper classes and leading men in the city to expel him and Barnabas. They *shook the dust from their feet in defiance,* and left their enemies in possession of the field. However, *the disciples they left behind were filled with joy and the Holy Spirit,* so even those neoconverts acknowledged meaning in that maelstrom of jealous rage. For all of them, meaning came in the person of

Jesus Christ. His human history is the pattern of our human history. The meaning in His life makes the meaning in our lives.

Knowing Jesus as the *firstborn of many* leads directly to the fourth quality of a joy-filled Christian life: a humbled sense of continuity with all of humanity. Taught by the Holy Spirit, we know that we somehow live in solidarity with all peoples. We are not atoms floating through history; we share own individual existence with others—with the church as it thrashes its way through humankind's truculence, with this nation struggling to keep possession of its soul, with this city and this neighborhood.

Joy-filled Christians experience this solidarity in utter contradiction to the alienation, isolation, and narcissism of our postmodern culture. Hence we have in some particulars repudiated the culture that we inexorably took into ourselves as our own, because our culture is marked—stained—with alienation, isolation, and narcissism. We are correct to understand this process as a very important part of *dying to self*. Any Christian who lives joyful has taken the means to escape the bitter dynamics of alienation, isolation, and narcissism, and if he or she has not found an effective means for complete escape, then has recognized the situation as a share in Christ's suffering. He did everything He could not to be alienated from anyone, or isolated—and then suffered both, bitterly.

To feel solidarity with all peoples is a charism, actually, of those who have a deeply matured faith in the Incarnation and in Christ's Mystical Body. Each of us knows himself or herself unique before God, as Jesus did and does. All of us also know ourselves children of the same Father and *members one of another*. Anyone who really knows all that does not need to be told *Rejoice*.

So there are the qualities: Joy-filled Christians have taken responsibility for our own lives. We accept that we belong to God and feel a deep harmony between what comes into our lives and God's creative love. We live serenely convinced that human life has meaning, and feel keenly that we live in solidarity with all people.

Let this be a little footnote, a sort of warning printed in small letters on the label: Perhaps *Rejoice* is not the way God is dealing with one or other of us. Perhaps; some holy people have lived a kind of lifelong martyrdom. Nonetheless, any prolonged sadness—Teresa of Avila called it "the eighth deadly sin"—generally indicates that we have some decisions to make about our selves and our lives. Certainly, no sad event or experience excuses us from looking for this joy in our lives, or from begging God for it when we seem to have lost it.

This may all seem complicated enough to make us groan or laugh. We should choose to laugh. It may be that this is a fifth quality to the joy-filled life, anyhow: laughter. Jesus' life must have been full of laughter. Otherwise, little children would not have climbed all over Him. And if Jesus did not laugh, why would one of His first acts have been to gather disciples and lead them to a party in Cana? Why, when they ran out of wine, would He have made more? Jesus laughed. People didn't flock around Him because He was uptight and dour.

Rejoice in Him. *I say it again. Rejoice.*

A lot remains to be said. Thomas Aquinas, for instance, claims that joy follows immediately upon the acceptance of God's love for us.

Of course, if we do live joy-filled lives, God will have achieved it in us against considerable odds.

Each of us has finally to decide for ourselves whether we think that people who live joy-filled lives take themselves seriously. And how seriously?

Prayer

Lord God, we are glad
to bless Your holy name.

We are glad to say yes to our self
whom You are making,

and glad to take responsibility for our self,
for all we have done and all we have failed to do.

We are glad that we belong to You,
who have made Yourself our God,
and us, Your people,
and we are glad that You pour out on all
the Spirit who comes to fill all our ins and outs
with happy meaning.

We are glad to join ourselves to all peoples,
to embrace with You their sufferings and joys,
their hopes and fears.

We are glad
to trust that You will crown Your work in us
with the peace of the Kingdom of Jesus Christ.

We are glad above even that
to be able to say that we love our God and Savior,
Jesus Christ, our Lord and good brother,
who is glad to go on living in our humanness,
who already reigns with You and the Spirit
forever and ever. Amen.

10. A Man of Honor

He took his wife to his home.

How should the messianic age begin? Left to our own imagination, we would expect this unique shift in epochs to begin, if not with sunbursts of fanfare, then at least noticeably. We would expect that some kind of event would make it impossible for anyone in the world to miss the fact that a totally new era in human history, the last era of all, had started.

The People of Israel thought that way at the time of Jesus' birth, and actually were expecting a rather spectacular inaugural of the age. Jesus Himself undoubtedly heard speculations about it during his boyhood: Yahweh coming in mighty power, all the nations quaking and trembling. During His public life, He had to face several popular myths about how the Messiah and the messianic age were to come. Some of the lawyers, for instance, thought that no one would know where Messiah came from, and others thought Bethlehem and others, Jerusalem. The guileless Nathaniel, when he first heard about Jesus of Nazareth, asked the sarcastic question, *"From Nazareth? Can anything good [for the kingdom] come from that place?"* Some people believed that no one would know who Messiah's parents were, which underlay the astonishment behind the question, *"Is not this the carpenter's son?"*

64

Jesus' disciples, like all of their contemporaries, had been shaped by the sense that the beginning of the new age would be fairly spectacular. They show that in their early preaching of the *Good News that God promised long ago through His prophets.* They give the impression of dating the beginning of the new age from the Resurrection, the moment *that the Son of God in all His power* broke back into human history, as Paul wrote twenty-five years after Jesus rose (second reading). They also went back and forth on the question whether the endtime would come promptly and complete the beginning of the new age, as though Jesus would have gone up to heaven and turned right around to come back down riding clouds and running up the volume of the music of the spheres.

By the time Matthew the Evangelist came to write, however, about fifty years after Jesus' Resurrection, the disciples had begun to measure the age's beginning differently. They had clarified for themselves the truth that Jesus Christ had been Son of God from the moment of His conception. They had come to understand that Christ's life encompasses the lives of all who believe in Him, and that He spreads the messianic age less like molten magma from under Vesuvius and more like flowers' fragrance through a house's rooms. They found themselves thinking that, as the messianic age is the age of God incarnate, it begins with intimately human affairs.

Matthew, therefore, does not envision the age beginning with *the sight of the terror of Yahweh, the brilliance of His majesty.* He envisions the age beginning instead with an invisible quickening in the womb of a young girl. So he puts first among five prophetic citations about the Messiah this mysterious promise written by Isaiah: *"The Lord Himself will give you a sign. It is this: The maiden is with child and will soon give birth to a son whom she will call Emmanuel"* (first reading). This delicate, lovely event alone marked the very beginning.

Matthew applied this prophecy to Jesus Christ. Isaiah, critics contend, may have understood something else by it, or even several things. But he surely meant to assert that a Davidic king would one day appear who would make definitive changes. This king would embody in his own life and action a decisive intervention by God our Lord into the people's history. He would take the final steps in establishing the messianic kingdom.

He was surely to be David's descendent, but also in some extraordinary way *God-is-with-us.*

Matthew meant to assert all of that. He also wanted to assert very clearly that Jesus of Nazareth was David's descendent, and to achieve that he wanted to establish beyond cavil that Joseph, descendent of David, accepted Jesus as his own son. That established, he could justifiably record Jesus' genealogy as a descendent of David in the manner of genealogies in Genesis and Chronicles: *Abraham was the father of Isaac... David was the father of Solomon... And Jacob was the father of Joseph the husband of Mary; of her was born Jesus who is called Christ.* It is not necessary to point out that Matthew did not have to invent anything in order to establish as fact that Joseph took Jesus as his own son. He did no more than report what Joseph succeeded completely in doing. When Jesus stayed behind in the Temple, his mother asked Him to *"see how worried your father and I have been, looking for you."* In Jesus' later years, people would know exactly who He was—*the carpenter's son.*

Matthew knew, however, from the stories circulating in Galilee about young Joseph's dilemma, that he had not succeeded without a struggle. *Before they came to live together,* he wrote, the girl to whom Joseph had been espoused *was found to be with child* (Gospel).

Joseph faced an anguishing situation. He and Mary had already been "married" as we would think of it, since their parents had closed the financial arrangements and made a formal agreement before two witnesses. Once *Mary was betrothed to Joseph,* the full range of custom and of law governing the lives of married couples applied to their union. Mary would live at home with her own parents for a year or so, if things were as usual, until she was a little older than 13. In some areas, the espoused couple might be allowed to be alone for an evening or two; but that was not the custom in rural, somewhat fundamentalistic Galilee. That only made things worse.

When everyone began noticing Mary's condition, Joseph knew that the child was not his. MIBeing a man of honor and wanting to spare her publicity, he decided to divorce her informally.

Some commentators contend that Joseph knew from the beginning that the child had been *conceived through the Holy Spirit.* They believe that Joseph was simply too awe-struck and humbled to take Mary into his home. He was even afraid to do it. This is what Eusebius and Ephraem argued long ago and modern scholars like Xavier Léon-Dufour now argue. The angel had to come in order to allay Joseph's fears: *"Joseph, Son of David, do not be afraid to take Mary home as your wife."*

It may well have been that way, though it then seems odd that Matthew calls Joseph *a man of honor* instead of a man afraid. And why does the angel seem to be giving Joseph fresh information in the astonishing news that *she has conceived what is in her by the Holy Spirit?*

Perhaps it happened another way, a way more closely connected to the kind of man Joseph was: a man of honor.

Man of honor, as Raymond Brown points out, translates one of Matthew's favorite words, "dikaios," is its Greek form, which he uses nearly *20* times to mean something about being upright before the Lord according to the Law. In all likelihood, Matthew meant that Joseph was just like Zechariah, *who scrupulously lived all the commandments of the Lord and the observances of the Law.*

Joseph is reaching the end of his teenage as such *a man of honor.* Now suddenly he knows no more than that his espoused wife, before her year at home has passed, manifestly carries a child. He could not be the child's father. Knowing what he knows, the full weight of the Law in Deuteronomy 22 becomes stark grief. For if he were to take the Law as strictly as he tended to, he would be forced to denounce her and make her liable to stoning. At a minimum, he would have to go to her parents—not alone, but with two witnesses—return the marriage portion and dowry, and repudiate her before them.

Such a divorce would be *informal,* as Matthew puts it, but it would inexorably be very public. He would leave Mary to her parents and to her unwed disgrace. He could not take her home.

If we understand what Matthew is driving at, we should find this enormously moving. The Chosen One, from the time He is in His mother's womb, is entangled in the human labyrinth of custom and yearning, of consciences mulled by love, of Law fierce even in its beautiful order.

Joseph slept and woke, agonized and dreamed. *A man of honor.* Then, as *the angel of the Lord had told him to do, he took his wife to his home.*

Not long after that, Matthew the Evangelist says, *she gave birth to a son, and he named Him Jesus.* Jesus, of course, means "Yahweh saves."

The messianic age has begun. It is an age of our human life, a large division of years that memory can no longer sort out and number, an interminable succession of days down to our own. In certain crucial matters—honor, fear, nobility, hunger, safety, belonging—the pre-messianic days seem very little different from the new age. In the everyday matters of the human spirit, the days that have come after Joseph *took his wife to his home* hardly differ from the days that went before.

The only true difference encompasses everything else: Within the days and years of the new age lives *Emmanuel, God-is-with-us.*

He, too, has slept and wakened, agonized and dreamed, *a man of honor.* Just the same way as the man of honor who took Him as his own son.

The little we see of Joseph, David's son, reminds us how commonly God works in power when we are without resources.

If the last of all ages began so silently, why do we demand a circus of events before we will allow God to move us into a new stage of growth in Christ?

Perhaps the fathers among us should notice that the great, good man whom Jesus called father always did the next good thing and left larger outcomes to God.

Prayer

Sometimes we demand to know,
patient and gentle Father,
why we suffer and are confounded
who try to serve You in uprightness.
And You do not answer us.

Sometimes we find trusting You hard
because we believe that any great power
must act in notoriety,
demanding attention not only for its work
but for itself.

You, God, like the man of honor
whom Your Son called 'Abba,'
You work in infinite silence.

We acknowledge You, most silent God.
We adore You, humbled before the mystery.

And we beg that You open our ears
and unlock our hearts
so that we can hear and heed
the quiet coming of Emmanuel
and take Him to our homes. Amen.

11. Simple Answer

"Let what you have said be done to me."

Prayerful women and men through the centuries have been deeply impressed by Mary's response to the angel's message: *"Fiat! Let it be done!"* They have felt that the young girl heard God's summons courageously and answered it both prudently (*"How can this be?"*) and wholeheartedly. They have exhorted themselves and others to take the *Fiat!* as a model of the way each of us can respond to God our Lord's initiatives.

None of us would be inclined to argue theoretically against that assessment, though few of us feel it realistic to demand of ourselves that we imitate the Lady. We feel lacking in one or other, or all three, of the virtues Mary displayed—courage, prudence, and wholeheartedness. And anyhow, we do not often perceive God's initiatives quite as plainly as did the Mother of God.

Yet the saints—from Basil and Bonaventure to Frances Xavier Cabrini and Philippine Duchesne—testify that Mary does give us a real and feasible model. Perhaps reflection on the three things Mary said yes to will let us see her as a model.

Mary said yes, first of all, to being a mother, to generating another life in her own self. She said yes, that is to say, to regenerating in another all that God had brought to be in her own life. Without meaning to imply that this young girl was a transcendent genius, uniquely wise and perspicacious among humans, we can say that Mary's whole self rose in jubilation at the possibility of reproducing the divinely graced human life that she exulted in. Her "Magnificat" does not express a joy at high and unimaginable gifts alone; it exults in seeing the light of day and hearing the harmony of nature's sounds and feeling the textures of things.

To say in our current jargon that Mary "felt good about herself" would be to make a hopeless understatement. The fact is vastly profounder. Mary said yes to all of her concrete life and all of her actual thoughts and desires before she said yes to reproducing human life in another. Her yes to everything in her experience—keep in mind that this woman never once disrupted her proper relationship with God the Lord or with those whom God had given her to love and to be loved by—precisely made her the unique candidate to reproduce the human life that came to be as the Son of God.

It is the Lady's first yes—to her self in its giftedness and limitations, to her history and the stages of her growth, to her lifeworld's religion and politics and economy and culture—which we must imitate first. If we do not imitate that yes, then we cannot imitate any of the rest of her yeses. For regeneration means generating again out of a life what that life has come to be filled with and to mean.

Regeneration is always a mysterious and wonderful process. It was uniquely mysterious in the case of Mary's pregnancy, because the Child she consented to bear and rear was to be *the revelation of a mystery kept secret for endless ages* (second reading). How would she know when to chide and when to cherish such a child? How would she know when to form firmly (as she surely had to do) and when to give scope to His exuberant spontaneity?

She would have wondered in timid anticipation like any expecting mother, and with better reason. Nonetheless, her yes to motherhood was wholehearted. When she said it, new energies coursed through all her bloodstream and along all her nerves and sinews. For she said yes to new life in her self. She had no image of the unseen, all holy God. But her fantasy and even her sinews imaged forth into her self the beginning of this sacred new life.

Why can we not say such a yes to the new life of God within us? Of course we cannot imagine God. Of course we cannot envision what future our yes will bring, not even what the moment after we have spoken it might bring. Yet we can say a yes from our heart and from our blood, from our memory and from our spirit. When we do, we have modeled our yes on the Lady Mary's.

Then, second, even as she said yes to becoming a mother, Mary said yes to living a virgin. In this, she was responding to God's initiative of self-donation. For God begins the cycle of self-donation by giving Himself. Astoundingly, He waits to give Himself to this little girl until she has accepted His Gift. Here dwells the profoundest of mysteries. God humbly asked a little girl whether she would consent to give herself to Him alone, entering a nuptial union whose literalness makes the mystics' claims seem merely metaphor.

We have to be careful not to retroject into Mary's religious experience what humankind has learned from her Son and from His Spirit. Mary knew God only in faith, only under that strange opalescent light on human experience, even after she felt her body physically swell with the infant she had conceived. She models here many things in our lives, not just the most extraordinary.

For we experience constantly the works of the Spirit of Life, even knowing in our own bodies what we know we could not spontaneously cause to be. And yet, we know the Spirit of Life only in this strange way of knowing called faith.

Mary's yes to remaining a virgin is a yes to following God's initiative even when she could have no idea where it would take her and her life. That kind of yes, every single one of us must say not only at important junctures in our lives, but constantly even in little matters.

God knows that we are dealing here with mysteries within conundrums, far beyond the grasp of our minds. For God chose that His Son be born into this earth's cycle of life apart from the usual exercise of genitality. In that way, His Son's conception and birth prefigure the kind of self-donation that each of us will know in the Kingdom. For when the Reign of God has reached its fullness—as we understand this matter now—we will live enfleshed and enspirited as by nature we already are. Yet there in the Kingdom, we will *neither marry nor be given in marriage.* And there we will know the most complete and fullest joy our human frame can contain. How these things can come about, we do not know.

We do know, however, that they have not come yet. All of us still live our sexuality and most of us live our genitality. For to some, God's initiative comes as a call to virginity or to celibacy; to some, God's initiative, as a call to physical union and to parenting.

Whatever His call, God's initiative invites full self-donation from all of us. For in the last analysis, our yes must be to whatever God summons us to be. We cannot say a yes with our whole self to that which our self cannot attain—and still please God. Neither can we say yes to very much less than our self might attain—and still please God.

We can see in this, thirdly, how Mary said her yes not only to motherhood and to a way of life, but to becoming as a self. For she said yes to the self that God was drawing her to be, however incomprehensible that self— both virgin and mother!—appeared to be.

So do we all say yes to the self God is creating in us, a self probably as replete with apparent contradictions as virgin-and-mother seemed to be. We say yes to a self that we cannot now fully know, a self mysterious even when we can think most clearly about our history and our life.

In the end, we cannot really dodge the choice whether to say the kind of yes that Mary said with prudence, courage, and wholeheartedness. For if we mean to acknowledge God as Creator, we can only echo what she said —*"Let what you have said be done to me"*—whether or not we have the slightest grasp of what that entails.

This means giving to God a simple answer: Yes from my most intimate self to all that has been and to all You want to come. It confounds all of our wisdom. Ultimately, it confounds all human wisdom, altogether. Mature disciples recognize that this yes itself is a gift from the God of Life. Our place now is to say it when we can and when we feel hesitant or unable, to ask earnestly for the gift.

One conclusion emerges quite clear: When we say yes to our self and to our life history, we say yes at the same time to whatever now comes.

We might wonder why anyone who does not exult in his or her own life would want to generate a child. We might wonder even more what that means in the child.

Mary's fiat entailed trusting God first and in a unique way, but it also entailed trusting Joseph and her own parents. So does every great fiat any one of us must say entail trusting God and, always, others.

Prayer

Almighty and courteous God,
so kind are You,
and so beautiful Your project in the world,
that we might expect ourselves to say our yeses
with our whole heart and spirit,
courageously launching out in trust.

You have known, Lord of passionate love,
that we have turned our prudence
into timidity,
covering over the exulting desires
Your Word summons up in us
with inane hankerings and hesitations.

We ask You, from Your throne above the angels,
let the eternal ringing of the Lady Mary's fiat
stir You to create in each of us
all the little yeses that You hope in us
until we come to say the thunderous yes
with all Your holy ones for endless ages. Amen.

12. Consolation

Blessed is she who believed that the promise made her by the Lord would be fulfilled.

In most prophetic literature, the Messiah emerges more like an impersonal force or a super-hero than like someone we might understand. And His mother is simply referred to as *a maiden,* nothing particularly personal. Even in Isaiah's Servant Songs, in which Yahweh speaks tenderly of *"my chosen one in whom my soul delights,"* the Messiah appears more a symbol than a person. In one line, He says of Himself that *"Yahweh called me before I was born, from my mother's womb he pronounced my name,"* and in the next that Yahweh *"made my mouth a sharp sword."* Real person or real symbol?

Yet, Jesus and Mary both lived intense interior lives and they left vivid instances of what that life was like. They even made it plain that from day to day they lived in what spiritual writers call "consolation."

Consolation? That means that they were interiorly at peace and continually able to believe and hope and love God the Lord. It means that they were inclined simply to do the next good thing, leaving to the Creator the larger definition of their personalities. They were spontaneously disinclined to do anything wrong or even apart from the Spirit who moved them, leaving to the Creator things they found beyond their control. To them, whatever was good seemed pleasing and inviting; whatever was evil, ugly and repulsive. So they lived in consolation.

Within that consolation, Jesus and Mary acted in freedom, in assurance, and in obedience. Those three qualifiers of their way of acting tell us a great deal about the way we are called to act, so we should look at each in turn.

To begin with their profound freedom. Mary showed great freedom in asking how she was to conceive a child without intercourse. Scholars from St. Jerome on might not have felt that they had in hand a kind of movie version of how Almighty God and His handmaid communicated. But scholars and people of deep prayer have been altogether clear that Mary did not swoon or squeal. Mary communed with God from the full dignity He had given her at her conception. She let no fear block her yes, and no phony "I am not worthy." Once Mary was clear about what God asked of her, she said simply, *"Fiat."*

In that moment, she is the queen-mother. Many queen-mothers would sit at home working away at their dignity, as would many a dauphin. Not this woman. When she heard that her elderly cousin Elizabeth was pregnant and about to give birth, pregnant herself, she *set out in haste to the hill country,* leaving so few details for Luke to collect that she gives the impression of total freedom.

In the same way, Jesus acted with such freedom that he gave heartburn to those who needed to wrap themselves in law and custom. It was not the fact that He violated stern custom, for instance by healing a man with a withered hand on a sabbath right in synagogue, that shook the lawyers. What shook them was that Jesus felt such mature freedom when faced with any and all religious strictures. What they really ought to have noticed was the freedom with which Jesus faced life's limitations. Even as He faced the final conflict, Jesus insisted that He was freely laying down His life, *"no one takes it from me."* We give medals of honor to those who act like that.

Secondly, Jesus and Mary lived with great assurance. Their assurance did not abstract them from everyday realities, and make them live somehow detached and diffident. Nothing could be further from what we are told about them. This Israelite man and woman lived assured of God's favor in their own time and place and in the sometimes contrary circumstances they woke up in. Mary could hardly have felt overjoyed to have to go down to Bethlehem with Joseph just when her baby was due. She simply went. Faced with assertive religious leaders, Jesus spoke His penetrating truths without any of the stridency or mental gymnastics that marks the less-than-sure mind. The two of them once found themselves at a wedding when a wine shortage deeply embarrassed the host. With perfect assurance, Mary made a mother's suggestion to her son; with perfect assurance, her Son on His own initiative advanced the timing of His works of power earlier than the time set by the Spirit whom He obeyed.

Their assurance was not a passivity. On the contrary, their assurance before God was precisely a readiness to find in each new day what the history of their relationships with the Father would bring next. They were confident that they would find what they wanted to find. Mary astonished Elizabeth with her assurance *that the promise made her by the Lord would be fulfilled.* Before she left her cousin after *about three months,* her body gave evidence that her assurance and her trust had been justified.

Her Son learned this assurance from her so thoroughly that we could not readily find a parallel to the assurance that Jesus moved in all His life. He summoned disciples, and after prayer selected twelve quite common men to spread the Good News *to all the earth.* As He preached, He constantly used phrases such as, *"I assure you,"* sometimes *"solemnly."* Jesus was sure He could command spirits and fevers and He acted in that assurance. He was sure that He spoke only the truth, so that those who heard Him experienced that *He spoke with authority.*

In later years, he would confidently speak on a high mountain with Moses and Elijah *about His passing which He was to accomplish in Jerusalem.* After a little time of prayer while His three most intimate friends watched and waited, His whole body radiated with evidence that His self-confidence was justified.

Toward the end, He came to know that one of His twelve closest co-workers was planning to betray Him. He felt assurance in Himself that He would be able to face and bear the consequences of that betrayal. At their last supper on Passover, Jesus quietly said to Judas after he had taken the holy bread, *"What you are going to do, do quickly."*

Jesus' personal history unfolded within the context of an explosive combination of religious, political, and national currents. They finally pulled Him under. Such was His union with God that, even in this contradiction, He could say to Pilate with perfect confidence: *"You would have no power over me if it had not been given you from above."*

This quiet confidence in God marks the person who obeys God. This raises the third way of acting in consolation.

Jesus and Mary obeyed God, and the way they obeyed God grew out of and contributed to their consolation. Neither of them ever experienced a kind of stoic resignation to "God's will," as to a sort of impersonal force. Rather, they knew God in all the circumstances of their lives. They found in their own consciences and in what their lifeworld dictated to them, not God's will as implacable demand, but God's loving care as invitation to life growing to its full.

Jesus, it is true, said Himself that He had come *"to fulfill the Law, not to abolish it."* He told John the Baptist to wash Him because that appeared the right thing to do at that time. And when Jesus came face to face with the *prince of this world,* He told His friends, *"He has no power over me, but the world must be brought to know that I love the Father and that I am doing exactly what the Father told me."* He sounds there almost like a young soldier punctiliously keeping the commands given him by a much-loved captain.

Yet Jesus gives plain evidence that *"what God told me"* does not mean that He received commands the way a tape recorder takes dictation. Jesus and the Father carried on a dialogue, each taking the appropriate initiatives. In the Garden, Jesus allowed some of His friends to overhear a small moment in this dialogue. Jesus and the Father had already come to decision: Jesus would *"lay down my life."* But when He reached the moment to enact His free decision, Jesus' human frame was intolerably stressed and He turned to the Father in this new circumstance of leaden dread and physical revulsion, asking Him to review their decision. He clearly was not an automaton; He saw obedience as a dialogue between truly independent persons. But He expected the last word in that dialogue to be the Other's. He obeyed.

Even in His obeying, He did not become mechanical. Had He wanted to, He could have continued the dialogue of the Garden even after he had been arrested. He could have appealed to the Father, He said, and the Father *"would promptly send more than twelve legions of angels to my defense."* He did not make that appeal and freely carried out what He and the Father had chosen.

Mary's obedience, judged by the less explicit information that we have of it, functioned that same way. She obeyed God in becoming mother, but not without dialogue. She obeyed God by rearing her child in such wise that He would never as a baby feel alienated from her on the one hand, or on the other feel smothered and over-possessed. Each of those excesses, to which parents are prone because of our sinfulness, would have exposed her own son to sin. Consciously obeying the full range of maternal instincts woven into her self by a God who both mothers and fathers, she let her child go, even when that meant standing under the gibbet He hanged upon. Mary's obedience was the obedience of waiting and of being there, and God *the Father of all consolation* filled her spirit with profound peace.

Plainly, to conclude, Jesus and Mary led their lives in consolation. Their consolation, however, had nothing to do with treacly sentimental religiosity, or with a life free of worry or wart. It corrects our mistaken tendency to think of consolation as cheery naivete or as vacuous unconcern.

Very much the contrary. A life of consolation means a life charged with labor, since *the God of all consolation* Himself works busily *wanting nobody to be lost.*

Any person who leads a useless, purposeless life goes through its years in the most desperate desolation, no matter how prettily painted and cos-turned. Here is the deepest spiritual root for the drugs, incessant travel, and glutted consumerism of those who live without God.

Christians who live over a volcano of rage or in a desert of depression (barring psychiatric disorders) need to have a look at what they truly believe and hope for. And whether they have chosen *the freedom of the children of God* to live joyful with the gifts God pours out on them, or the freedom of the marketplace to take the pleasures they want and demand that those pleasures make them happy. And whether they have felt assurance from money and power or from the creative love of God. And whether they have obeyed God or instead acted like mindless bureaucrats filling in the forms, or like petulant children demanding their own way.

A life of consolations means acting in great freedom, and with great assurance, obeying the Spirit speaking in our hearts and in the Church. It means an earnest determination that *now His greatness shall reach to the ends of the earth,* at least to those ends nearby (second reading).

To this consolation, each of Christ's disciples has a right. In it, in fact, each of His disciples is summoned by God to live.

In the end, we have to step back and ask candidly: If consolation does not always mean feeling good, why would anyone try to live consoled?

How can anyone live in consolation whose lifeworld has shattered— children away from their faith, spouses divorced, jobs terminated?

If we are called to live in consolation, and if consolation entails a kind of freedom and assurance and obedience that we feel lies beyond our powers, then the consolation of God must be a gift.

Prayer

Lord God of mercy
and Father of all Consolation,
we know Your gift and doubt we have it.
We know our birthright to a life of joy
and hesitate to claim it.

Righteous God, You know us:
how instead of enacting our true freedom
we bind ourselves in fashion and groupthink;
how instead of acting out of the assurance of the Spirit
we crave insurance against what we name failures;
how instead of obeying You in grateful dialogue
we act as though Your will were Chance or Fate
we act as though You Yourself were a wayward Force.

No more, God of Consolation; no more.
Against the forces in our lifeworld
filling us with anxiety that we are inadequate
driving us to frenzy lest we miss what others make
pressing us to pour ourselves out like salesmen on shoes
against all these forces
we concur in Your consolation.

We choose the freedom of enacting our own consciences.
We choose the assurance that comes with Your spirit.
We choose to find You caring for us
in all the circumstances of our lifeworld
and in all of our commitments.

We choose to give to You the last word
in the dialogue that is our lives. Amen.

13. He Gave His Word

The Word was made flesh; He lived among us.

There are more majestic feasts in the church's calendar than Christmas, and more solemn ones; but no feast is warmer or more suffused with quiet light. It is a gracious time that much of the world shares, Christian or not; a time when Scrooges miraculously mellow and lots of God-less people grow fond of one another for vague astrological reasons written in their stars.

Christmas' warmth, however, does not have to be mere seasonally adjusted sentiment. Not for anyone, and certainly not for thoughtful disciples of the Lord.

For there are several sources of its warmth.

Partly—this would be a source for everyone—the warmth flows from the celebration of the renewal of human life, in this case, by a birth. Any birth seems fine because it is a gratuitous continuation of human life, a gift to all of us from a mother and a father who have enjoyed and appreciated their own lives. The little infant, everyone hopes, is living evidence of their abiding love for one another. Certainly, an infant fills us all with a kind of atavistic confidence in the reality of that abiding human love—a related source of the season's warmth.

For those who are at least marginal Christians, the contemplation of Joseph's concern for Mary and of Mary's for her Son is part of the warmth of Christmas. The memory of the concern felt by strange and wonderful wise men and by homely shepherds adds its peculiar warmth. Christians have been remembering all that since at least some time before 336 A.D., when an illustrator with the wonderful name of Furius Dionysius Filocalus drew up a list of feasts that included: "December 25, natus Christus in Betleem Judeae." Representations of the nativity scene ever since radiate a rich gentleness and an earthy kindness.

For more reflective disciples of Jesus Christ, an even deeper source of warmth comes from our recollection of whose birthday it is, anyhow. The Jesus who lies represented there in (nowadays) plastic splendor is *Wonder-Counselor, Mighty-God, Prince-of-Peace.* Down through the centuries, the reflective have pondered the mystery that we have tenaciously clung to: *In the beginning was the Word. The Word was with God and the Word was God.* It fills our hearts to think that *God so loved the world,* our world of wounded humanness.

For nowhere apart from the creche is it clearer what world God loved and—we are taught warmly by gazing at the scene of His birth—still loves. He loves the world of humankind as we know it in our lifeworld, as we live it and make it up. Surely, it is part of the warmth of Christmas that Jesus was born in the middle of a foul-up in census-taking, the kind of foul-up we all know only too well, with nowhere to sleep, let alone to get born. So He enjoyed a beginning that speaks loudly of God taking to Himself the whole of human experience—dignity and indignity, orderliness and muddling through.

It is in this familiar world of ours that *God's grace has been revealed.* Those of us who maturely live God's gift recognize that we are getting close to the profoundest source of the warmth of Christmas: God gave His Word. This *free gift* coming to us in God's Son gives us the utterly secure guarantee that God's mercy will indeed outlast the sinfulness of humankind.

We learn a truth here we need very much in our day: We are not to imagine that we could irretrievably blow into radioactive dust His beautiful handiwork of this earth, because now He has made concrete His promise that we *who enjoy His favor* shall live an eternal *peace.*

It isn't as if the people had had no secure guarantee before Jesus' birth, of course. God the Lord had made a covenant with the people, step by step pledging His faithfulness to them, continually affirming to them that *you will be My people, and I shall be your God.* He pledged to them not only that *all the ends of the earth shall see the salvation of our God* as spectators, but that through Israel, His salvation would *be for all the peoples.* And God has indeed achieved that, whether the people at a given time remained faithful to Him or not.

It is true that the people were bound to keep their side of the covenant, and all the Jews in the world still are. That is their glorious destiny. It is also true that they have not been in the past any better than we are now, who often enough still earn the scathing rebuke Isaiah puts into the mouth of God at the very start of his book: *The ox knows its owner and the ass its master's crib; Israel knows nothing; My people understands nothing. They have abandoned Yahweh... They have turned away from Him.*

But all along—back in the time of the prophets and kings and now in the time of the pontiffs and theologians—God the Lord has committed Himself and made the ground for mercy God's own fidelity. *It was for no reason except His own compassion that He saved us.* As Pope John Paul II has written in his encyclical *Rich in Mercy,* "when two parties pledge their goodness to each other, they are faithful to each other by virtue of an interior commitment, and therefore also by virtue of a faithfulness to themselves."

It is not for your sake, O House of Israel, that I am about to act, but for the sake of My holy name. If that humbles us, it also assures us that some power other than our own worthiness binds God our Redeemer to us. Any of us who have sense will rejoice that we do not have to find some unshakable quality or excellence in ourselves that binds God to us in total fidelity. That unshakable quality and excellence are in the Lord.

Here we are at the deepest root of Christmas's warmth: the enactment of God's forgiving love in our own lifeworld. God's mercy is like a woman's love for her child, "completely gratuitous, not merited," the Pontiff writes. The little creature in a woman's womb can merit nothing; everything is given to it. Well, *does a woman forget her baby at her breast, or fail to cherish the son of her womb? Yet, even if these forget, I will never forget you.*

This turns out more than just a splendid, heart warming image. God's commitment is not some new intention added to His already infinite goodness. The stunning truth we contemplate on Christmas lies in this: God's commitment dwells in a living reflection of God's own Self, and has dwelled there since before time was. What is new comes with God's forming the times and expressing His commitment to humankind by giving His own Word. *The Word was made flesh; He lived among us.*

With that, the reason why God will be merciful, indeed *the God of all mercies,* has shifted ground. And the reason for Emmanuel, why *God-is-with-us,* has similarly shifted ground. For what moves God to mercy—in God's own being, in God's own "experience"—grows not only out of the divine nature, but now also out of human nature, taken up into God in the Person of His Son.

That bears repeating: *There is a child born for us, a Son given to us,* and now the goodness in God which grounds His infinite mercy to us sinners is the goodness of our own human nature. Anyone who can find no warmth in that makes old Scrooge seem about as flinty as playdough.

Another way of saying why Christmas glows warm in our hearts: Even while creating us, the Lord of history takes three initiatives, the first of which wipes out the force of our sin and renews our life.

God's second initiative sends into our flesh the eternal Word, so that our Salvation out of our ruined humanness resides within it.

God's third initiative re-consecrates all of creation. Jesus, who embodied as well as announced the Good News, felt the same nourishing tenderness toward children, the same wonder at flowers and figs, as we feel. Redemption in Christ has the fragrance of warm bread, of full-bodied wine, of a Christmas tree.

Prayer

Almighty and every watchful God,
You compare Yourself for your tenderness and care
to a woman with her baby
and to a father with his child.

We would never have dreamed of You that way.
Humankind never has, anywhere, any time.

We thank You and we praise You
for revealing Yourself to us this way.

We acknowledge You almighty Creator
because we see the works You accomplish around us;
we acknowledge You tender parent
because we hear the Word You have spoken in us.

Lord God, as we gaze on Your Son born of woman,
let this *Wonder-Counselor* create in us God's own mind.
Let every child, woman, and man we encounter
remind us how You give us grace on top of grace,
since Christ fills our humanity with the divine Presence
who is *Mighty-God and Prince-of-Peace.*

So when we grow to feel as Emmanuel feels
then will Your Word spoken in us
fill our lifeworld to all the ends of the earth
with the warmth of Your love. Amen.

14. Naturally a Celebration

"Listen, I bring you news of great joy, a joy to be shared by the whole people."

What is the *joy to be shared?* Who make *up the whole people?*

First of all, we celebrate and share the joy of an historical event, Jesus' birth. It is an historical event as well documented as Augustus Caesar's birth, for instance, and a great deal better documented than, say, Buddha's. As an historical event, Jesus' birth affected history profoundly, as did the births of Alexander the Great and Confucius and Albert Einstein. It could quite reasonably be argued, in fact, that Jesus' birth taken simply as an historical event affected human history more than that of any other child born of woman. Set aside what His birth means and look only at externals—at political events, social forms, artistic products, scientific developments, and scholarly works. Arguably, more of these of greater consequence unfolded among those committed to remembering His birth than among those committed to remembering any other's.

So all of us celebrate this fact. Those who believe in Him and those who are unbelieving all acknowledge that human history as recorded by the race was decisively shaped by this birth.

Of course, that decisive shaping might have been disastrous. A lot of people in what we tendentiously called "mission lands" found excellent reason to think so in the way Christian conquerors and missionaries acted. Some speculative thinkers in Christendom itself have thought Christianity disastrous, whatever they thought of Jesus' birth. The acerbic Voltaire did, and the despairing Nietzsche. However, they had convictions stronger than the evidence they based them on.

For the case is different, and we have this joy to be shared with all humankind: Jesus' birth has had an overwhelmingly positive effect on the course of human history.

We can hardly review two thousand years in a few sentences, but we do not need to. With no attention to chronology, and intending not to demean other civilizations, we can note that western civilization has been the cradle of scientific inquiry, technology, printing, constitutional govern-ment, electronic communication, genetics, modern democratic govern-ment, immunology, flying, medicine, mass production, atomic physics, mass marketing, and a lot else that makes up the postmodern world. We can note further that very many of these developments, particularly in their beginnings, were created by men and women under explicitly Christian impulses.

A Catholic monk, to start with this instance, began the science of genetics. Moveable type was first used to print the Bible. The first known secret ballot—surely an improvement over election by ordeal—was cast by the college of cardinals.

We might feel impatient with some legalities in Christian marriage at present, but we need to remember that Christians are the ones who shaped marriage into a contract in which the woman had some rights—more and more as the centuries wore on. In fact, what we now call the "women's rights movement" itself began and flourished in the Christian West. And if we are impatient that we took so long to get women into higher education, we need to remember that the first universities were launched by the church and only the Christian West has democratized higher learning

(learning, not technical training, which is better democratized in the Soviet Union than in the West).

It was Christians who shifted from mere conquest—an inveterate human custom—to the "age of exploration," feeling compelled to take the creed throughout the world. Even though they were driven by very mixed motives, explorers and missionaries carried with them a mindset that of itself kept pressing for equality among all peoples and for a community of nations. Long before supra-national corporations and the United Nations, the church had developed into a truly world-wide organization, encompassing peoples on every continent. The current "world village" owes a great deal to the village of Bethlehem.

The democracy we know in the twentieth century grew in Christendom, steadily motivated by Christians' sense of the equality of all before God. That self-governance inexorably spread beyond merely an elite, to which it had been limited in Greece and Rome. It was a profoundly Christian leader who proclaimed "government of the people, for the people, by the people," intending to include those of every race, color, and religion.

It is strange to recall that atheistic Communism began in a Christian context; Karl Marx did his research and writing in a library collected by good Christians. This partially explains the oddity of Communist North Vietnam drafting a constitution modeled on that of the United States.

Such a convoluted phenomenon raises the reality of the inner history of humankind, of how we perceive and conceive and explain. We do not have to make definitive arguments about historical causality before we can say simply that this, too, has been profoundly affected by the birth of Jesus.

So we disciples celebrate *this news of great joy:* that He divides the history of human interiority in two. To begin at the deepest level: Before His birth, humankind yearned to live forever, but our hope lay beyond our grasp. Only some force outside of our selves could make us live forever, a force other than our own life. We were living contradictions—beings with a focusing impulse to keep living forever, whose life could not of itself go on forever. Since His birth, both the yearning for eternal life and the power to achieve it rise up from within existential humanity. Hope has dawned within our own human life of a way to live—our own enspirited flesh and not some shadow or pale remnant of it—forever. Jesus' birth made that possible. As Paul wrote to Titus, *God's grace has been revealed, and it has made salvation possible for the whole human race* (second reading).

His birth originated other deep changes in human interiority. Before Him, the noble-minded grieved hopelessly at human vileness, rejoicing gratefully only at the permanence of the sun's splendor and the predictable glory of lilies in the Spring. Since His birth, humankind has learned to trust more and more wholly what is in the human self. We are not forced to rely for betterment on the pseudo-permanence of the sun and the lying persistence of lilies; we do not need magic or the influence of the spheres. We do not have to define progress in terms of science and technologies. We have been enabled to rely optimistically on the splendid promise of the human self. No wonder the Christian way is marked above all by joy!

Before His coming, people ran to the Great Spirit in rare consecrated places and ran dreadful risks from other spirits everywhere else in their *land of deep shadow* (first reading). They stood helpless with terror when God visited them in the violence of wind and earthquake. Since His birth, the people bestow consecration on every place they are present in, temple or hearth, desert or laboratory. And we know that "natural disasters" change nothing but geography.

Relevant to this inward change in human history, it was in the Christian West, not in the China of many calendars, that Galileo conceived heliocentrism. It was in the Christian West, not in an Orient so fascinated with the workings of the human mind, that Freud found the freedom to investigate the inward workings of the wounded human spirit.

We celebrate these profound human changes at Christmas in celebrating Jesus' birth. We correctly consider them a part of what He came to introduce into the world, "to share my joy with them to the full." But we do not celebrate them only.

For if Jesus' birth has transvalued every human experience, paradoxically the whole point of His being born at all was to save each human person while leaving human experience intact.

So, finally, we celebrate the joy of human experience as God keeps on summoning it. We do not breathe a different air since He came, or digest differently, or think and communicate angelically without image or word. It was to breathe the midnight air of David's hill-town that He was born. It was to digest our food that He came—to break bread with family and share a cup of wine with friends. He does not displace our minds and our memories; it was to bring divine power into human words, and to bring a divine dream into human images, that He launched the thin, choking cry of the infant.

Once, the more truly human any became, the more surely they embraced silence and the time for death. Now, the more truly human any become, the more surely we embrace the Word proclaimed and its enacted promise of resurrected life.

No wonder the birth of Jesus, of all the events and beliefs the Church holds in honor, calls most naturally for celebration.

Looking at things from another angle, we might wonder what we would celebrate if Jesus had never been born.

Is it a temptation to wish that God in Christ had simply replaced with other ways the fallible human ways we follow?

Some cannot believe that it is the same Holy Spirit who moved Jesus to make the blind see and the lame walk; and moved Christians to invent, build, and care through all the centuries; and now moves the whole church to proclaim the faith that does justice.

Prayer

Lord Jesus Christ
when You came into our humanness
You did not seize a nature fully formed and finished
as in Your great power You might have done.
Instead, courteous and kind,
You came to grow in wisdom, age, and grace.

You continued respectful of our nature
when You came again as Risen Lord,
refusing to impose Your victory on humankind,
respecting the need we have to grow
and come through time to our full selves.

Yet in this gentle courtesy, Jesus of Nazareth,
You have blessed our humanity
as no other—none—ever has or could.

For You have done a work no other could do,
a work that now rests as an everlasting blessing
on each and every person
and on humankind all together
like the possibilities of the warm sun
on the fertile earth.

Come quickly, radiant Dawn of God,
and illumine all the reaches of our mind
and warm all the yearnings of our heart,

so that the dream of the Father in the Spirit
a vibrant kingdom of justice, peace, and love,
may spread upon us presently. Amen.

15. Thank God

The Word became flesh and made His dwelling among us.

Waking up as a child on Christmas meant instant hilarity, like hearing the name of an endearing character on Fred Allen's old radio show: Toura-loura Rabinowitz. For to the child, everything is wildly gratuitous; and to the child on a happy occasion, everything that comes seems rightly to come, and just as it should be.

As we grow into freedom by electing and choosing, we can lose that sense of life's gratuitousness and hilarity. "Thank God" very easily comes to mean about as much as "Amen" now means. Just a formality; nice, but a formality.

For us, then, who struggle to hold on to the sense that life is a gift and a wonderfully happy one, Christmas comes as a great help. Looking into the crib reminds us how freely God gives all of His gifts, and gives us occasion to ponder a couple of points about gratitude.

First, how we stand toward gratitude to God is a sign of the health of our faith-life. Living unthankful to God is like living with a low-grade fever, or going week after week deprived of enough sleep. Neither will prove dangerous in themselves, but both give danger signs that something is out of order in the body or in the whole self.

Living grateful to God, on the other hand, is like the glow of good health, when a person can handle whatever comes along easily. It means that we are receiving and accepting what comes from the hand of God. We are choosing to feel happily graced ourselves, and we are making God feel like a good giver. We are like the person who has been invited to a party and shows up in great good humor to enjoy the party and to draw others into enjoying it. That's gratitude.

There we have the truth that lurks behind a fairly trite exhortation: "Live the Christmas spirit all year round." That gem probably came from the mind of someone trying to get people to buy baubles during the January sales. Or was it to get people to give to charity? Whatever its origin, it's deceptive, because the real Christmas spirit is not the spirit of giving, merely. It is the spirit of giving gifts and receiving thanks, and also of receiving gifts and giving thanks.

On the other hand, the Christmas spirit is perhaps also a little more simple than the wisdom of some spiritual writers might suggest. For some writers suggest that the mature person rejoices not so much in the gift as in the giver, not so much in what is given as in the fact that anything is given. Well, no doubt mature persons do indeed reach that wonderful level of sophistication.

At Christmas, they might just have to lay that sophistication aside. Here's the second thing about gratitude to reflect on: At Christmas, we thank God in the first instance for what God gives us and we do not really do well to go much further than that. It is as though God wishes us to be like children before Him, for children do not get much farther than the gift given them. They get completely absorbed in what they are given. Their absorption is their gratitude (well, wise uncles and aunts think so).

At Christmas, if we understand the real gifts we are given, we are almost inescapably imprisoned in a kind of divine childhood. For Christ's birth—when we remember it in faith and in hope—reminds us of what we are by His gift: *His co-heirs, empowered to become children of God.*

Quite as really, God has given to us His Son. Any who try to get beyond the Gift here will quickly find themselves in a maze of conundrums. Just rest in the Gift, and say thanks.

At various times in the past and in various different ways, God spoke to our ancestors: in pillars of fire, in surprising victories, in the poetry of prophets (first reading). Now God manifests Himself in Jesus, so that the form of His self-manifestation is human. *God never said to any angel: "You are my Son, today I have become your father," or "I will be a father to him and he a son to me"* (first reading). God says that to this infant.

Our own entire humanness will never again become what it had been before His birth. For when God promised, *"I will write my law in their hearts,"* He did not talk merely of a moral law, a set of behavioral norms. Rather, God spoke of the law of His own life, a law of being, a new genetic code.

Here again is the form of God's gift to us: Jesus Christ's own human-divine life now originates from within human life the genetic code that guides its unfolding. Not of our bodies apart from our spirits, but of our whole enspirited flesh. Not of human life in general, but of each single human's life. *How beautiful on the mountains are the feet of one who brings good news, who heralds peace, brings happiness, and proclaims salvation* (first reading).

Look again at the infant and remember that all around are those who were regenerated *not by blood, nor by carnal desire, nor by man's willing it, but by God,* just the way this infant was begotten (Gospel).

There is our gift: In our own humanity shines out the radiance of His beauty, lovableness, delightfulness, of His justice and caring, of His divine life. Each person around us is somehow, as Hopkins put it in his great sonnet,

> "Christ—for Christ plays in ten thousand places,
> Lovely in limbs, and lovely in eyes not his
> To the Father through the features of men's faces."

In the final analysis, we are ourselves a never-ending succession of gifts of God. Even our gratitude is a share in His who never failed to start His prayer, "Father, I thank You."

What does this gift contain: The law that God has written in our hearts?

Could there be a gift with further-reaching consequences than this, that God has chosen so to arrange human life that whatever benevolent thing we do for any infant, we do for His Son? Or for any helpless person, or any stranger, or any beloved person?

Prayer

How in the night of our unknowing,
almighty and caring God,
You stole into our human flesh,
and with Your Son's gracious birth
abruptly wiped away our fecklessness,
we cannot now know well enough.

Still in our dreams, afraid to stand in Bethlehem's cave,
we know the nightmare of disordered love
out along the lonely plains of every day.

Still in daily things, our hearts hanker
for what cannot fill them,
and out of boredom we lurch into senseless battles
even with those whom we love.

Still in our prayers, with loud cries and lamentation
we protest that we sin and cling to it.

Save us, Father, from this unknowing night,
and bring us into the holy hollow where the Child lies.

Give us there to resonate deep in our spirits
with the harmonies of chaste self-giving
and of clean commitment.

Give us to live and move in this knowing light,
Your love that makes all of us Your offspring,
that steals softly into our own human flesh
and fills our loving with Your own. Amen.

16. Family Matter

Whoever respects his father is atoning for his sins; he who honors his mother is like someone amassing a fortune.

Mary and Joseph were the ones who first drew from the Child what He was to become. They chose, to take just one example, to encourage Him as He grew friendly with other children and to discourage Him when He showed the self-centeredness that all children have to outlive. He could hardly have grown into a selfish man or degenerated into leading a sinful life, since as Person He belongs in God. Still, He had in His human nature an enormous range of possibilities, each opening a different way of leading a deeply human, holy life, and perhaps each opening a different way of being Messiah. Mary and Joseph are the ones who drew from Him the kind of man He would become.

First of all, they drew Him to words. He who was Himself God's Word learned as infants do to make noises of need and of delight and then to make the sounds of sense. They gave Him the way He pronounced individual words and they gave Him the rhythms he used all His life of assertion and question and interjection. They led Him to know that no one person commands the meaning of any one word, and to experience how deeply these commonplace meanings connect us to one another. They would also have had to teach Him how laden some words are with emotional overtones and how some words evaluate what they name. They surely had to teach Him not to use the slang of prejudice.

So they taught Him words, and wove into His human consciousness their world of interpretation and of meaning. Jesus thought in the first instance the way His mother thought, and the way His foster-father Joseph thought. His valuing grew out of their valuing; His cherishing, out of theirs.

They also taught Him, therefore—or rather, showed Him—that acts, not words, are the stuff of love, and that as a consequence He need never despair of making Himself understood. And they showed Him how love always entails sharing. The deeper the love, the more all-encompassing the sharing.

In this way, second, they drew from Him ways of acting with others. If He was a uniquely apt pupil, He was a pupil nonetheless. He learned from Joseph, the man everyone thought His father, how men bore themselves in synagogue and how men acted when soldiers or tax collectors came around. He sawed wood the way Joseph sawed wood, and the chairs He made early on looked just like Joseph's chairs.

He learned from His mother how to wait patiently, a lesson He needed as the hidden years passed on. From her, He learned the prayers, such as those for lighting the lamps at the dinner table. He grew into her way of *treasuring all these things and pondering them in her heart.*

From both Joseph and Mary, He learned how to acknowledge in Himself who God the Father called Him to be. They did not know who He was to be, beforehand, even less than other parents know; they had to learn as He grew to His full self. Joseph knew that Mary *had conceived what is in her by the Holy Spirit,* and that he was to name the child *Jesus, because he is the one who is to save his people from their sins.* Joseph would have had no notion how Jesus could go about saving people from sins. So he simply did what he knew how to do and showed the boy the way to live gladly as a good carpenter and a good man (with the necessary adjustments, this is what every father does).

Mary had heard the promise that *He will rule over the House of Jacob forever*, the recollection of which must have puzzled her no end as He grew to boyhood and adolescence in Nazareth of Galilee, making roofs and furniture. Mary would have had no notion how Jesus could come to rule over Jacob, and simply did what she knew how to do and taught the boy to wait and always to react faithful to Himself (this may be the most important thing every mother does).

In the middle of all that, they did make Him able to know Himself and they encouraged Him to grow freely not just in age—who can avoid that?—but *in wisdom, age, and grace.* So when He reached the age of reasoning self-awareness, He began to take responsibility for Himself. Joseph and Mary even gave Him room to make His own mistakes, and He made at least one of the kind that are clucked over in any family for a generation or two. He remained behind in the Temple the year of His initiation, worrying the two of them nearly to death.

Even in that tense event—this is the third point—they were teaching Him how holy people do and do not judge others. The way they reacted when they found Him in the Temple showed Him that mistakes and externals are of no ultimate importance.

In fact, they showed Him that externals give no real measure of anyone's worth. We can almost hear Mary citing a commonplace as they entered synagogue, to make sure that Jesus appreciated her spouse: *"The poor man's wisdom keeps his head erect and gives him a place with the great."* That saying is in the book called Ecclesiasticus, written not long before Jesus' time; had already been in the Book of Samuel; and would later be in Paul's letter to the Corinthians. Joseph could very well have cited for his growing son another saying like it: *"Do not praise a man for his good looks nor dislike anybody for his appearance."*

Surely, too, they showed Him that suffering under tyranny diminishes freedom in grave ways; but considering all that they had gone through, they would also have shown Him that tyranny does not destroy the spirit unless connived in basely or responded to in embittered violence. For long before He faced a personal enemy (the story in the Gospel about Herod and Egypt means at least this much), He had lived intimately with a man and a woman who had faced personal dangers because of others' lust for power.

In sum, finally, Mary and Joseph drew from Him, from possibilities of which they could have had hardly an inkling, that combination of being from, of being part of, of growing apart—that combination that makes all of us children of parents and Him, Son. They achieved this with unique success. Even while they helped Him grow aware of His separateness, they kept Him aware of His oneness with themselves. Even while they elicited from Him the courage to separate His thoughts and convictions from their own, they invited Him to have the empathy to appreciate and cherish their thoughts and convictions. They never pressed Him to the point that He felt disgust with Himself or with them; He never as a boy stressed them to the point of feeling that they had become strangers to their own Son.

Joseph was not there when the final evidence came in that they had succeeded well in their parenting. It came as Jesus hanged on the cross. He had so deep a love for the woman who had borne Him that He wrenched His attention from His brutal anguish and turned it to her. Even in the deeps of a physical agony that drowned all emotion, He could feel how loath He was to leave her woeful, unbelonging, and unowned. He managed just enough concentration to get His best friend to look after her. In that final act, He showed how His mother and her beloved spouse had drawn from Him the only shape of human things which is destined to outlast time. Not prudence, not hope, not even wisdom; they will all be swept away as we enter into the mind and heart of God.

Before ever He could argue or doubt, and long before He gave His Great Commandment, they had taught Him how humans love and are loved. Had they not taught Him, He would not have known, as none of us does unless our parents show us. It is the only family matter of eternal consequence.

We know this is true: Parents give a child nothing who give the child everything except selfless love; parents omit nothing who give the child whatever they may have to give out of and with selfless love.

Anyone with sense can see how grace-filled for their children are parents' virtues.

Of all the troubles vexing family life in our day, one that must truly anger God is loveless parenting.

Prayer

How do we pray to you, Joseph, David's son?
How can we say out loud
that you are the father we all wish we had?

Listen to this and show us what to do:
We who are fathers and brothers in this culture
can barely claim our right
to nurture tenderly the children of our seed
and to love them gently.
None of us fathers any better than we are fathered.

In the face of that, Joseph, David's son,
teach us to decide and support so lovingly
that those whom we beget and love
will unfailingly wait upon the Lord and do His wish.

How can we come to you once again, Lady Mary,
to pray without formula or fakery?
Where will we find the courage to see you
as you are, strong woman,
leaving the pastel maiden of peachy skin and weak wrist?

Listen to this and show us what to do:
Our mothers and sisters are caught into a new generation
with no antecedents in womanhood,
so none of us mothers any better than we were mothered.

For all that, Lady,
teach us to wait in possibilities
and to choose so lovingly
that those whom we bear and love
will unfailingly become who the Creator hopes they will be.

Now can we come to You once again, most holy God,
Who have chosen to mother and to father each of us.
We ask that You teach us to wait and to decide,
to demand and to acquiesce,
until we have freely
let You make Yourself
All in all. Amen.

17. Sound Precedent

When the day came for them to be purified as laid down by the Law of Moses, they took him up to Jerusalem to present him to the Lord.

We are a people fond of innovation and invention. We can hardly bear having an earlier model of anything, or wearing last year's colors and costumes. Yet we cling to our Constitution and so successfully demand sound precedent in great affairs that our form of government has endured to become one of the very oldest on earth.

When it comes to our religious life, we are the same way. North Americans adopted the doctrines and practices of Vatican II quicker than we adopt tax breaks, and at the same time, we hold on to the Church's true doctrine so steadily that people in other nations claim to have the impression that we haven't any theology.

We therefore find something of interest in the event in Jesus' life when Mary and Joseph *took him up to Jerusalem to present him to the Lord* (Gospel). For we face a question of sound precedent in the wording of this passage. Some very old manuscripts say that *the day came for them to be purified,* and some others say *that the day came for her to be purified.*

Our translations of the Gospels reflect this division; some say *their* and some (usually the older translations) say *her.*

Most current biblical scholars are convinced that Luke wrote *their* and not *her*. They think that some ancient copyists tried to make that change because, with very limited information about the religious customs of the People of Israel, they judged that only the mother could be purified. Contemporary scholars understand that ancient impulse to write *her*, actually, because they are themselves a little puzzled by the *their*.

This scholarly puzzlement has produced serious research and pondering, taking us deeper into the significance of this story than we might have been inclined to go, and offering us a sound precedent in one very important matter in living Christ's way. Scholars' insights bear on what purification meant, who was to be purified, and finally why Luke used the plural *their*.

First, what *to be purified* meant to the people of Jesus' day.

We tend to think of any spiritual purification in terms of our Sacrament of Reconciliation, which is given us so that we can find forgiveness when we have sinned. But the people did not think of childbearing as a sin; they thought of it as a great blessing from God and a great service to the people. The Old Testament is filled with blessings on the wombs of those who bear children and constantly calls the man with children a happy man (unless, Ecclesiasticus observes, the children are badly reared).

The People of Israel were far from thinking child-bearing blameworthy. Hence, when the women who had borne a child went *to be purified*, they were not going to confession, as it were. They had not sinned.

What would serve as a good parallel in our practice for the Israelites' practice of purification? We could do worse than to think of purification as a parallel to our eucharistic fast. It is true that we keep only a token fast, just one brief hour. Still, we have tried to hold on to the meaning of it: We fast briefly before communion as a sign that we are leaving behind for a moment the things of earth's passing cycle and preparing to embrace the things of the eternal cycle of God's life. That is what purification meant to the people. Leave behind the things of the earth, like Moses taking off the sandals that accommodated his foot to the earth and John the Baptist washing off of penitents the grime of sinful living. Prepare for the awe of God's presence that burns but does not consume, that will bear no unholiness before it.

Though the belief was too complex to be stated briefly, we can correctly say that the people thought the opposite of *purified* was *unclean*. By that, they meant being immersed in earth's cycle of life. For instance, a farmer could do no plowing the day before he went up to the Temple, not because plowing was sinful or taboo, but simply because it belonged to the earth's life cycle of seed, growth, maturity, harvest. And again, Hebrew warriors abstained from intercourse with their wives before going into battle with the people's enemies, not because they thought intercourse sinful but because they perceived it as an act of the earth's life cycle. Warring for the freedom of the promised land, they considered a consecrated activity. They therefore abstained from intercourse before going to do battle with the power of God at work in their weapons and their sinews.

Not every purification was strenuous, of course; almost without exception, *to be purified* entailed little more than our eucharistic fast. Following the holy practice of her day, for example, Mary would have touched no consecrated thing for 40 days after the birth of her Son. She waited until she was physically and psychologically able to find some freedom from earth's cycle (beautiful as it is in re-creating life), and give herself wholly to God's.

We might get practical for a moment here. It is hard to believe that we would harm ourselves very much were we to recapture this concept of self-purification before holy acts in the cycle of Christ's life. We lost it in part because we have insisted that every action done by a *chosen race, a royal priesthood, a consecrated nation, a people set apart*, as St. Peter wrote in his encyclical—every action we do is a holy action. But we do not need to insist that every action is as holy as any other in order to guard the truth that our entire life goes forward "in Him, with Him, and through Him." Surely it does; but that every human act of a Christian is as holy as every other is no more the case than that every act between lovers is equally loving. Some actions—such as receiving communion or proclaiming the Word or teaching catechism—are holy in themselves. We might do well to prepare ourselves to perform them. Of course, if we do return to the concept of self-purification before performing holy actions, we would surely stop short of the odd tortures we inflict upon ourselves for the sake of being slim, or muscled in bulk, or successful.

All of us need purification in our lives, but we need to note here that, when a child came into the world, the Law of Moses required the purification only of the mother. This is the second point that scholars make.

The mother was to wait for a specific time and then present herself *at the Tent of Meeting... The priest is to perform the rite of atonement over her and she will be purified.* The passages in the Law to which Luke alludes—Numbers 8, Exodus 13, Leviticus 12—do indeed lay down that the firstborn son be *presented to the Lord* and *then redeemed* by some sacrifice. But the Law says nothing about *purifying* the child. Nor does the Law call for the father's purification, and neither does any tradition that has been recorded for us.

We might take occasion to notice something about the law in our own nation—the civil law. We have always kept reaching to make everyone "equal before the law," but during the present generation we have changed the meaning of that. More and more, we are applying every law to each person as though each person were currently the equal to all other persons—as though each person were a forty-year-old adult with solid education and heavy personal investment in the established order. We contend that high-school students ought to have the same freedom to print their adolescent opinions in schools newspapers as professional journalists have to report news in national publications. We try to pretend that women and men are equally involved in childbearing and rearing, meaning to erase all differences in their involvement. We let teenagers make unaided decisions about abortion as though they had the maturity to see what they are doing. In all of these matters, we face enormously complicated human questions, but we will face them more wisely if we remember how God treats each of us with equal love and kindness.

God deals equally with each person by finding that person where he or she is, accepting that person as that person lives now, giving that person the challenges and the consolations that the person needs now. This is what true equality before the Law ought to mean, and the equality that ought to be embedded in the Canon Law as well as in the civil law. The Deuteronomic law did that.

The case we are talking about here shows it: The Law required the mother to be purified, but not the father. Hence, we are justified in finding some significance in the fact that Joseph and Mary both took the child up to the Temple. This is scholars' third assertion.

For Luke's *their purification* does not refer to Mary alone, and can not refer to Mary and Jesus. While no scholar would want to press the significance of this too far, *their purification* suggests that Joseph consciously chose to share with Mary the ritual uncleanness connected with the birth of Jesus. He entered with his whole heart into the truly splendid cycle of pregnancy and birth and early infancy. He immersed himself in that beautiful cycle of earth's life. Following that out, he meant to join her in purification.

Together, then, they went up to the Temple to be purified and to offer to God a pair of turtle doves, the sacrifice of those *who cannot afford a lamb,* as Leviticus puts it.

The point to notice is the mutuality. Whatever ritual prayers may have been spoken over Mary alone, she and Joseph both accepted that for a time they both had been absorbed in the affairs of this earth's life cycle. Now they both needed to re-dedicate themselves to the Kingdom's life cycle, and to take once again the leisure to enliven and vivify their relationship with God the almighty Lord.

They found no special precedent for this in the Law or in their people's practice, as far as we know. Instead, we can justly say, they set a precedent by their own attitude and action.

This beautiful mutuality between Mary and Joseph should be no surprise: Everything Jesus touches becomes mutual in some profound way. After all, the Son of God receives from the Father everything that He is and has, and in their turn they share all with the Holy Spirit. And after all again, the Son of Mary and of Joseph the Carpenter learned how to live mutuality and to share from the heart from the two people of all on earth who knew best.

So their mutuality should be no surprise. Still, it is good to note that the current instinct among Christian couples and Christians in general to live more and more deeply mutual has this sound precedent.

In this day of self-realization, psychotherapy, and hightech personality training, what would a mature Christian intend by some self-discipline for Christ's sake?

In this day of communication, bonding, solidarity, and togetherness, what would a mature Christian intend by mutuality?

In this day of faith and justice, of divine immanence, of transforming human life, what would a mature Christian intend by purifying him or her self of earth's cycle of life?

Prayer

Lord Jesus Christ,
there are many things you could have done
with Your great power over nature and the human heart,
and many things you yearned to do.
But You did not force Jerusalem to gather under your wings.
You did not force each of your companions to remain loyal.
Or force the rulers and the money changers to act justly.

Instead, You waited to find out what each one needed
and even what each wanted
before You gave them what You could.

Everything about You, Lord,
proclaims that all we are is shared

and all our love meant to be mutual,
not talked about but done,
and always the giving back and forth of all good things.

This is how You came and shared with us
what we are and have and have done.
This is how You come constantly and offer us
to share what You are and have and have done.

We wonder at how uneven it is, Lord,
for You know that we haven't so much to give,
only our self.
We wonder that You are content with what we are and have.

We declare to You,
if You will give us the heart for it,
we would embrace whatever purifying we need
in order to live content with Your self-gift
and in order to learn
to make our own to You. Amen.

18. Crisis in the Family

Three days later, they found him in the Temple, sitting among the doctors.

Not many of us have been centurions or had a withered hand, so when we are asked to enter into the experiences of such people in Jesus' life, we just do our best. But all of us have been in a family, or still are, and we feel a sharp immediacy when we enter into the experience of the boy Jesus staying behind in the Temple. We feel the build up of trouble *when they were on their way home after the feast,* leaving the boy back there in the city. We mentally wring our hands at the picture of Joseph and Mary *looking for him everywhere,* for two entire days and part of another. For everyone has been on one side or another of a child's guileless self-assertion.

When we think about it in our times, we see that Mary and Joseph trusted a social structure—whole villages commonly traveled in company to and back from Jerusalem on the three feasts that required a Temple visit—and that social structure failed them. It was simply not encompassing enough to fence in the brave zeal of a keen 12-year-old, who may clearly grasp an obligation but cannot always accurately reckon consequences.

So a man and a woman search in anguish. They search for their first and only son. They search for one on whose life tremendous promises depend. And then a clear-eyed youngster suddenly sees the pain in their gaze and feels His compelling reason to linger sputter out into white-faced sorrow at what He has caused them.

Incidents like this are common in family life during any age. And in family life right now, incidents of mutual anguish are multiplied because of seriously inadequate social structures. Families today are like a shoal of dolphins in polluted waters.

Christian families do not escape any of these dysfunctions, for none of us fails to take into ourselves attitudes and ambitions woven into our culture that make it harder for us to be successful members of our Christian families. We suffer from developments bad in themselves and good in themselves; we suffer from the changing role of women, mobility, weakened public education, dissolved neighborhoods, consumerism, the drug culture, and a lot more.

In fact, the ills that every American family has to work through hurt Christian families in special ways, because they put tremendous stresses not only on our morals, but on the deepest truths we know about ourselves as persons in Christ. We might take each of these considerations in turn: the troubled family, the Christian family response, and the relevant truths about person in Christ.

The troubled family did not make the news just recently. It was a major concern of those who contributed to the Bicentennial bishops' hearings a dozen years ago. It was a top priority in the Call to Action that came out of those hearings. In fact, the American bishops named 1980 the Year of the Family and launched a 10-year program to revitalize Christian family life.

But the troubles in family life are not troubles just among Christians, and they are not liable to respond easily to efforts among ourselves. The data is plain: The divorce rate continues grim; the number of one-parent households has increased by a third during the last decade. One recent survey indicated that one of three school children now lives in a one-parent home. We are so appalled by the numbers of battered children that we have passed laws making it a civil offense for an adult not to report even total strangers for doing it. We are unnerved that mere adolescents get "sexually active," as we put it now. We are told by some social psychologists that we fear children and have discarded all the customs that helped us bond them to ourselves and learn to love.

The things that trouble family life reach beyond numbers and are structured into the attitudes prevalent in the nation. Narcissism makes us attend anxiously to our "self-realization" and to "doing our own thing." Nothing pressures us to a "family-realization" and just the names of some family virtues seem quaint or ominous, like "family loyalty." And yet at the same time, we suffer a kind of intimacy-imperative, a need to communicate about more and more intimate matters, and to share at deeper and deeper levels. This seems a beautiful development, but it can be a serious trouble to any couple who merely respect and honor each other and live serenely loyal, but who have no gift for, or call to, incessant mutual psychologizing. In marriage today, the deed done seems not good enough; any "really good" marriage has to be analyzed.

And, of course, our culture imposes a driving need—it is much more than a revolutionary freedom—to start early and stay late in genital activity and to achieve a kind of sexual athleticism. Sex has become a consumer item. It gets mixed in with all the other consumer goods we are driven to accumulate, so that genuine family communion gets smothered by heaps of gadgets and garments, and drained away by the latest fad in activities.

These are all things we know about, structures which make Christian family living very difficult. Yet we cannot avoid buying into them to some serious extent, so that every one of us contributes to the structures themselves, to the very things that cause our families problems. We need to keep mindful of that fact when we turn to solving the problems in our family life.

This raises the second point: some Christian responses. The mere fact that each of us creates the problem as well as the solution should set off an alarm bell. It means above all that in our nation we find it very difficult to reach the tranquil selflessness that we must believe characterized the life of the Holy Family. Where is the tranquility in American family life? Where is the selflessness? When television wanted to portray a family that lived tranquilly and generously, the writers had to place the family three generations back, in a golden age now long gone. Programs that portray current family life are full of broken people and braying asses.

Yet those qualities that Paul listed for the Colossians, *heartfelt mercy, kindness, humility, meekness, and patience,* will have to characterize any home in which the faith is truly being handed on (second reading). Merely stating that in our day suggests a mindset that is out of touch or at the very least totally countercultural. Probably the Christian mindset about family does require of us that we go against our culture in important ways, but no one who tries to live family life can stay out of touch for long. Sooner or later, one of the children will stay behind in the Temple, inflicting anguish and requiring forgiveness. And if we cannot *forgive as the Lord has forgiven us,* then our young will never learn how the Lord has forgiven us.

Put it another way. Even in this country of individualism, our virtues are not for ourselves; they are for one another. What Paul says about peace, for instance, is true for every virtue: *Christ's peace must reign in your hearts since as members of the one Body you have been called to that peace.* We have been called to every virtue *as members of the one Body,* and in truth we practice no virtue as solitary, unembedded persons. We might practice solecisms or crotchets. But virtues are endowments of the social person, the person inextricably interconnected with those whom God has given us to love and to be loved by.

This being for one another itself militates against all the dysfunctions in American culture. But it is not just a moral imperative. It is not just a fad, either, like TM. Being for one another is not a fine religious practice, to finish the matter, like enthroning the Bible in the home. Being for one another flows from everything we are as persons.

This raises the third, somewhat abstruse, point about being persons in Christ. We were told as children that we are made in the image and likeness of God. Then later we learned that God is not one Person, but three

Persons. Each of these truths is a profound mystery, but mature Christians will consider how they are related.

We are made in the image of three Persons whose entire existence is a shared existence, each of whom is this Person because of relationships with the Others. We do not understand much about the divine Persons, but we can understand that somehow we exist as persons the way those Persons exist. To speak very exactly, we are made in the image of the Second Person.

We exist insofar as we are related. "Self-fulfillment" therefore cannot mean something like filling up a glass with the best wine around, a kind of solitary perfection that has to come before loving others and accepting love from them. First you fill the glass and then someone can drink from it. No; self-fulfillment must mean something about coming to appreciate and approve and assert the selves in a loving union, a kind of communal maturing that comes to each even while it comes to the others. It means something like filling up a word with its full meaning. For a word is nothing but physical sound unless it has meaning among us. Then when one of us speaks a word, another accepts it in the sense in which it is meant, so that now the word has its full meaning—once there is a sharing. That's true self-fulfillment—always mutual.

This is very difficult to understand, but one thing ought to be fairly clear. The Great Commandment that summarizes the whole of God's way and His project for humanity's future expresses everything that we are as persons. When we live out that commandment in substantial ways, we simply undercut all the structural problems that plague our Christian family life.

Of course, we are finite and everything about us is finite, even our acts of love. So each of us will eternally be the child of our mother and our father; each of us will eternally be brother or sister. There lies the first love, and the first self-fulfillment. There must be the beginning of belonging, of self-giving, of accepting love.

Why would we be surprised that each disciple of Christ first learns the most important human lessons within a family? It was in a family that our

Master learned them, even when He made the kind of serious miscalculation that provokes a crisis in any human family.

Looked at this way, the Christian family promises far more than it might were it merely a convenient social structure or a useful moral training ground. Isn't the love rooted in the family what we are made for?

Some might mistakenly think that, if its members truly love God, a family will escape being hurt by the current crisis in the social structure of family life. Didn't Jesus, Mary, and Joseph truly love God?

We might note that the parents and the Son did not resolve their misunderstanding. Even this very holy family had to offer full-hearted forgiveness when they did not fully understand.

Prayer

Spirit of the Living God,
You hovered over the Virgin Mary
and she conceived.
You filled Joseph's spirit with wisdom
and he took her as wife and reared her Son as his own.
You filled their home and their life
with patience and goodness and tenderness.

Then we confess that we are puzzled, Holy Spirit,
why You would lead the parents to trust the Son
to so loose and fallible a social structure as group pilgrimage,
and why you would inspire the Son to remain in the Temple
without their consent and without even telling them.

We are always inclined to hope
that You will so fill our minds and hearts
with openness and harmony and peace

that we feel no tensions among our selves
but enjoy already and manifest the perfect harmony of the Reign.

We declare before You,
Lord of Light and Spirit of holy compassion,
that we do not demand that holiness and wholeness.
Instead, we accept as enough what You teach us:

For those who love God, all things work together to good.
Not even a sparrow falls apart from God's governance.
God our Creator knows and numbers the hairs on our head,
cherishes the inches of our height,
and tenderly measures to us the days of our life.

In all our crises and all our hurts,
We will trust that You hover over us
and dwell within us,
letting nothing escape You,
shaping our lifeworld and our selves
in the fullness of Your mighty wisdom and power.
For You live and reign forever and ever. Amen.

19. Stand Up Straight

As for Mary, she treasured all these things and pondered them in her heart.

As the night began to give way to dawn, *the shepherds went back, glorifying and praising God for all they had heard and seen.* They drifted around the town, telling everyone about the brilliant light and the splendid message and the little Child. *Everyone who heard it was astonished* (Gospel).

Through all of this wonderful activity, Mary moves with graceful serenity. In the translation of one scholar, *She kept with concern all these events, interpreting them in her heart.*

This graced stance of hers, *keeping with concern* and *interpreting in her heart,* positioned Mary to go through all kinds of turbulent events with serenity. This same stance is a grace offered to us. For her Son learned it from His mother, and then modeled it for us. More than modeled: *God has sent the Spirit of His Son into our hearts* (second reading), to mold us in the image of Jesus Christ, and to teach us to move as Mary did with graceful serenity through every kind of event in our lives.

We might find Mary's modeling of this charism more useful right now than a dozen New Year's resolutions, which we seem to take mainly for

119

the purpose of humiliating ourselves, anyhow. Her graced stance has three moments.

First, it brings the ability to stand alone. Mary was alone at the Annunciation. She had to be; each human must make alone those personal choices that confirm the deep structures of a unique human life. She made her choices alone, each of which turned out to be a generous self-donation, first to God Himself, then to the One to come, and in the end to all with whom she shares humanness.

We have to be aware, however, that her aloneness was not lonesomeness, which is the painful absence of someone beloved. Nor was it loneliness, which is the agony of alienation from the Other and from others, the painful missing of someone, anyone, whose name the lonely do not know. Her aloneness was, rather, the power of the maturely independent to elect interdependence, the power shared with us by God so that we can choose to love.

In that mind—and this is the second moment of Mary's graced stance—she discovered in herself an unshakable confidence in God. She knew with her whole being that God masters circumstances in which we can see no meaning, such as the death of innocents and the political disappearance of good people like her cousin, John the Baptist. Even more than that: She knew that God rides in mastery over events in which we can see only madness or chaos.

Mary could *keep with concern all these events* because she fully expected that her conceiving—and the census, the angels, the shepherds, the whole of it—would make perfect sense in the long run. She *kept all these events,* wanting to forget nothing, because God had authorized it all. She employed to its fullest the power of trust given to us by God so that we do not have to select among real things what to remember and what to try to blot out. We do not have to un-remember even our worst personality traits, or our most embarrassing blunders, or the harshest hurts inflicted on us. We do not have to un-remember our sins, suppressing ugly infidelities in the hope that somehow they will make no difference. Of course they have made a difference and still do; our confidence is that the difference they make will not ruin us. By the power and passionate love of God, we are saved out of it all and redeemed from all sin. For the sake of gratitude and hope, we *keep all these events,* not like a storage disk of data, but *with concern* that we live grateful for all of the gifts the Lord has lavished on us.

Anyone who thinks about Mary's story knows that she had to wait for some of it to make sense. Perhaps her longest wait stretched through a *great sabbath,* when she had nothing to go by but her hope. She would not have despaired, though, because she was able to interpret the events of the sabbath's eve enough to keep her hope alive.

Here is the third moment of Mary's graced stance: It gave her the power to interpret events as far as she needed to at the time. She did not snatch her child away from Simeon and Anna, or brush aside their prayers as the maunderings of doddering old fanatics. She took in what they said and waited to see what it would come to mean. This strong woman did not grieve that her Son left her to go and preach. If she followed Him, she was not chasing after Him with a bowl of soup; she was following Him as a disciple, learning (which is the way Luke, who knew most about Mary, portrays her). Mary did not faint and collapse under the cross; we are told explicitly that she *stood there,* up straight.

Mary could manage these situations because she could see as much sense, could interpret enough, to do the next good thing she was called on to do.

We are summoned by God to accept in the Spirit this same graced stance: the power of independence that allows us to love; the power of trust that allows us to act; the power of interpretation that allows us to endure.

We need only fulfill one condition in order to accept it fully. We must *keep with concern all these events, interpreting them in our hearts.* Perhaps we've come upon the only important New Year's resolution: We will remember what God has given us in the year just past and in the whole of our life so that we may be grateful for it, all of it. Then, out of that recollection and gratitude, we will interpret for the coming hour and day the next good thing we are to do. The shape of the new year and of all things to come, we leave in the hands of God.

The simplest among us can follow that program, which will keep the wisest among us busy. All of us will find in it the way to move through our lifeworld in gracious serenity.

We never end pondering this: We are made in the image and likeness of God not only relating eternally as Persons, but somehow also One God and unutterably unique. So therefore is each of us.

We are never finished pondering, either, the events and happenings that give shape to our life. For each of us must decide whether we can sanely believe that an infinite power governs them all.

In this day of teeming madnesses, it is a truly great gift from the Spirit of Life to have the sense that some meaning shoots through it all. That sense of meaning is a gift, and cannot be earned.

Prayer

We give You thanks, heavenly Father,
that You create each one of us unique,
measuring out our growth through a genetic code
You write into each cell of our body and in no other's,
and mark out the day when we are born
and the day when we are born again,
and number the day on which we will enter
into the fullness of Your life.

We give You thanks, eternal Word of God,
that we are coming to be in Your image,
who trusted the Father
as totally as birds trust the air,
and enacted Your own freedom as confidently
as a grain a wheat set in the soil to bring forth life.

We give You thanks, Spirit of the Living God,
that You accept every gift from Father and Son
of wisdom and understanding and knowledge,
and that You bear these gifts so freely into our hearts,
coming as gently into our lives
as meaning dawns in our minds.

We give You thanks, who are one and only God,
that as each moment begins
You call us to stand in Your presence and serve You.

Come quickly and uphold us or we shall be broken reeds
windblown by absurdity and selfishness.
You alone can make us stand straight,
for You are Lord forever and ever. Amen.

20. Your Light Must Shine

Arise, shine out, for your light has come.

G. K. Chesterton once pointed out that almost no one thought the day of Jesus' birth in any way out of the ordinary. That, he said, was extraordinary, since on the day Jesus was born the entire universe turned inside out.

Before Jesus' birth, humankind turned upward and outward to face God. People had to look beyond earth and beyond human existence to find God. After His birth, we are no longer to look upward and outward to face God; we are to look horizontally among ourselves. We do not have to look beyond earth and beyond human existence, but into a cave instead, and into all the ordinary human things that belong to the church of God.

Actually, this reversal was not without antecedent; it had gotten something of a start in Jesus' own people. The People of Israel were to look closely into themselves, into their own history as a people, and find God working there. Hence, Matthew began his Gospel with the genealogy of Joseph, David's son, majestically counting back through the generations to David and then to Abraham.

Matthew intended to help the People of Israel look into their own history so that they could see how God gave Himself more and more fully until He came as *Emmanuel, God-is-with-us*. As the writer of the Letter to the Hebrews began: *At various times in the past and in various different ways, God spoke to our ancestors through the prophets; but in our own time, the last days, he has spoken to us through his Son.* The earlier times were in a true sense just a foreshadowing of these last days, which see the substance of God's self-donation to humankind.

Matthew the Evangelist had pondered the people's history in just this way. Precisely within that sacred history, he recognized Jesus' birth as both miraculous and epochal. Hence, when he set himself to write Jesus' life story, perhaps fifty years after the Resurrection, he depicted the birth as altogether extraordinary, whoever had or had not noted it at the time. Matthew, at least, recognized the truth of Chesterton's observation that the universe had been turned inside out. For this is the birth of the Son whom God *has appointed to inherit everything and through whom he made everything there is. He is the radiant light of God's glory and the perfect copy of his nature,* as the Letter to the Hebrews says.

That same letter cast Jesus in the role of the new Moses, a theme which Matthew had already raised. For he brilliantly lay the story of Jesus' infancy onto the frame of the people's exile in Egypt and the exodus out of bondage. He wrote: *This was to fulfill what the Lord had spoken through the prophet: "I called my son out of Egypt."* The prophet meant that the People of Israel were called out of Egypt by the Lord, so that the whole People prefigure the Messiah. The whole people prefigure the Mystical Body of Christ, and we currently embody on this earth the eternal life of the Son of God.

The world has been turned inside out for all of humankind, however, and not just for the People of God. Perhaps that is why Matthew takes Jesus' genealogy back only to Abraham, suggesting that now it is through Jesus Christ that the people will come to be more numerous than the sands on the seashore. For by telling the story of the visit of the Magi, Matthew weaves into Jesus' infancy the proclamation that a new covenant has been offered to humankind and the work of redemption extends to all (Gospel). As Paul had already written to the Ephesians, the Gentiles were invited to count themselves among the people of God, because *now the same promise has been made to them in Christ Jesus* (second reading).

Here is another place where the entire world has been turned inside out. That promise made in Jesus, God-and-man, means that the light we are to see by no longer comes from outside the electric blue planet, from outside the human heart. As Isaiah had elaborated the promise, the light comes from within: *Arise, shine out, for your light has come... though night still covers the earth—and darkness, the peoples* (first reading).

The point is that the light no longer glows down on upturned faces; now, the light glows within human hearts, into which Christ and the Father have poured the Holy Spirit. *Now you too,* Paul wrote to the Gentiles in Ephesus, *have heard the message of the truth and the good news of your salvation, and have believed it; and you too have been stamped with the seal of the Holy Spirit of the Promise.*

To those who comprehend its full meaning, this gives intense hope. However, it also draws the attention of anyone with a grain of sense to another truth: We already know all we need to know to give complete human shape to the world. We know what God hopes for our selves and for our lifeworld. In a very real sense, we are where the Light comes from. At this point, parenthetically, just in case the matter might have gotten too mystical for those of us who have one or two grains of sense, we might recall who said, *"You are the light of the world."*

Well, what's wrong?

Mahatma Gandhi, asked why he was not a Christian, said he would be if those who profess Christ lived what they claim they believe. G. K. Chesterton, as everyone over forty knows, put it another way when he said that humanity had not tried living a fully Christian life and found it wanting. The truth is that we have not wanted to try it.

That really is the problem, and Jesus knew that it would be. He left to His disciples the task of witnessing to the new covenant, of shedding the light of the Holy Spirit upon the unbelieving world. So He warned His disciples, intending that we in our day and time should overhear: *"Your light must shine in the sight of all."*

In the last analysis, this is the tough truth: If the light of Jesus Christ is to shine on those around us, it will shine through each of us.

This truth hides another tough truth: The faith and the virtues of Christians are given them not for their own salvation alone.

Here is perhaps the toughest truth of all, for it is about the church that we know. With all our struggles and pluralisms, the church must attract humankind to want membership in the Mystical Body of Christ. This might suggest some reflection on our attitude toward the church.

Prayer

Oh, Lord,
when You sent Your Son among us
You sent into our own humanness the Light
that alone can lead humankind into your kingdom.

He has handed on to us through all the generations
the ministry of reconciliation
and the mandate to make His light shine out.

When we look around at ourselves
we do not feel encouraged that we can shine out
so brightly in our lives and in our loves
that those who do not yet know your Son
will come to love Him
and those who do not yet know His salvation
will come to yearn for His gift.

So we ask You, great Shepherd of all our souls,
to raise up among us good leaders
who under the guidance of Your Holy Spirit

can remind us of what we need to know
and give us courage to do what we need to do.

And when You raise them, Lord,
raise up in us good companions and followers for them
so that Your church in its own life
may come to be a great light shining
to attract to Your Son the whole of humankind. Amen.

21. Wise Princes

Some wise men came to Jerusalem from the East.

American Catholics have not been known for their devotion to King Yazdegerd of Saba, whom sixth-century Syrians numbered among the three magi. We do count three magi, though, adding one to the pair who gaze from the wall of a Roman catacomb and whittling down the dozen listed in an enthusiastic medieval manuscript. We also think of the three as kings, the way the sixth-century Syrians did.

Right after Vatican II, though, we almost quit thinking of them altogether. Parents with children in catechism class left Melchior, Balthasar, and Gaspar in their tissue wrappers along with heirloom blown-glass ornaments. We were intimidated by—or perhaps enthused by—apodictic chatter about an implausible star. We all learned what "midrash" means, and how the sacred writers had used mythic illustrations to get their message across without intending to write literal history as we know it. Battle-wearied monsignori snorted and grandparents got hives.

The mythic regicide of the three magi, church history will record, was something of a hallmark of the ultraliberal fifteen and twenty years ago. Some who had only recently discovered that exegesis was not a geothermal blowout put the same kind of exuberant faith in it as the discoverers of plastic put in it, with similarly excessive results.

129

They prove to have been too enthusiastic in "disappearing" the kings. They taught all of us, it is true, to be more careful of what we say about them. Matthew, for instance, does not call them kings (Gospel). He does not say that a vagrant Betelgeuse left its appointed place in the heavens and dipped close enough to earth to trace a path. He does indeed "say" that Jesus appeared, was ignored or rejected by some of His own people and recognized and given homage by some Gentiles.

But Catholics are not even furtive any more while placing the three kings in the creche. We have simply gotten clearer than ever that we are celebrating a humble human event dressed up in a regal splendor that signals its inner reality.

Above all, we understand that Matthew was bringing the glory of the natural world and the splendor of natural human wisdom to *do Him homage* (Gospel). There, we have learned an important lesson from the story of *how some wise men came from the East* to Jerusalem.

For while the first Chosen People had the prophets and the Scriptures to teach them about God, the Gentiles have had only nature. They did not have a poor teacher; Paul explained to the Romans that *ever since God created the world his everlasting power and deity—however invisible— have been there for the mind to see in the things he has made.* Those who are both wise and good are likely to comprehend that evidence and follow it like a north star to God's house. Their wisdom and their goodness both belong to nature and are indeed manifestations of the wisdom and goodness of the God of nature. So of course in Matthew's story it was from nature—the natural wisdom that Paul talks about in his letter to the Romans—that the magi learned about *the infant king of the Jews* (Gospel).

This is worth noting by those of us who *were not a people and now are a people.* For ordinarily, people are drawn to God and to His Christ through the things of nature. Not through the splendors of the snowflake and the balance of galaxies, merely, but through all things that are of nature. We might fret about church people getting politically active and theologians writing sociology. We might wonder why missionaries spend such a great deal of energy improving people's diet and giving education to the ignorant. We would wonder that way, perhaps, because we do not notice that political processes, social status, diet, and literacy are things of nature. They belong to the natural world as truly as do snowflakes and galaxies.

Putting some reasonable order into humankind's affairs—so that the hungry are fed and the ignorant taught and those vexed by illegitimate government find some relief—putting some order in all that simply makes nature more transparent. It makes the evidence of God's work in the world clearer, and the traces of God's own Self clearer. And if Christians accomplish that ordering, then it also makes our witnessing to Christ's new covenant more persuasive.

All of that helps the "magi" still abounding in our world to *see His star as it rises and to come to do Him homage.* They will not see a roaring ball of diamond light drawing pilgrim roads over the rolling earth. They will not see things that overwhelm their reason and ravish their freedom to choose. The first magi of all never saw anything like that.

They will see none of that because they are not seeking for a God who works that way. Instead, they will see "the little green leaves in the wood and the wind on the water," to cite the famous passage of hopeful agnosticism in Archibald MacLeach's drama, *J.B.* Only now they will see everything with new eyes. They will see signs of love where before they had seen only eagles and roses, and see meaning where before they had seen only phenomena.

So when the church turns to those nations and peoples who still do not know Jesus Christ and brings them, or helps them find on their own, the current equivalent of *gold, frankincense, and myrrh,* we are only taking a lesson from the stars. Not from the galaxies, but from the mythic stars among Christ's worshipers, the magi.

And we may just as well call them Melchior, Baltazar, and Casper as anything else. For somewhere back there were real people, persons just as memorable as each of us and just as readily misplaced by history, who chose to acknowledge that Jesus is Lord.

Now instead of gold, frankincense, and myrrh, we bring to Christ medicine and instruction and institutional care.

Why do we hesitate so much to take the stars as models for our behavior? What holds us back from saying simply that we would like to act like Thomas More or Philippine Duchesne or Dorothy Day? We ape the notorious readily enough.

The people of the United States have been notable for their experience of God in the splendors of nature. That has sometimes been misprized as secularist or contrary to established religion, but has God the Creator canceled all the evidences of Himself in nature?

Prayer

We praise you, Lord Jesus Christ,
for the company You keep;
for the little girl who gave You birth
and the carpenter who reared You.

We praise You that shepherds gathered You in
and fishermen hauled oars for You;
that stonecutters made cathedrals to honor You
and pilgrims journey still to the land You walked upon.

We praise You that kings knelt to Your Cross
and queens embroidered it on their mantles;
that cities march on Corpus Christi day
and whole nations celebrate Your birthday.

We praise You that You have willingly traveled
to all the nations and to all the peoples;
that You have continued down through the centuries
making friends of all the willing.

We praise You that You have absorbed Your friends' gifts
and passed them on to those who needed them;
that You prefer for company
those who need.

We declare to You, Master of the Magi,
we are those who need;
and we prefer being numbered among Your company
to being kings over the whole earth. Amen.

22. Secret Plan

They were overjoyed at seeing the star.

Astrologers from the East arrived one day, Matthew wrote, as though Mary and Joseph never knew who would drop in next. In his day, the East stood as the symbol and the source of wisdom. In our day, that same East—particularly Iran, which covers the area the astrologers might have come from—stands as a symbol and a source of conflicting and somewhat insane ambitions.

Iran hardly stands alone, of course; conflicting and somewhat insane ambitions harrow every corner of the world. What do the peoples want? Can we even know our own desires? Pope John Paul II wrote that humankind's confusions are worsened even by our best and most cunning innovations. We seem unable to steady ourselves even in our desiring, now wanting one thing and again another—often enough its opposite.

We do not even know what to desire before God. As Paul wrote, *we do not know what to ask for as we ought.* This above all the flaws in our desiring illustrates how deeply wounded we are by sin and error, and how total our need is to have God's Holy Spirit teach us what to want.

Now, at one time, it seemed as though the Spirit would teach not all of humanity, but only a chosen part of it. In this last of all times, we celebrate

134

annually the event of the Epiphany, when God revealed that the Holy Spirit is to teach all peoples what to yearn for. The Epiphany reveals God's secret project in desire: that all people will come to want from the depths of their selves the Reign of God.

This is a complex matter, so here are just three more basic considerations.

First, Yahweh Elohim taught His chosen people to desire a land of their own where they could serve Him and live in peace, a kingdom of plenty with a perfectly just ruler and a genuinely just social order that cared for the widow and the orphan and would not allow bad luck in weather to deprive a farmer of his land. But even as God taught the people to yearn for that promised land, He also gradually taught them that Israel would be a light to all peoples. As Isaiah put it, though in the present *darkness covers the earth, and thick clouds cover the peoples,* the day will come when *the nations shall walk by your light, and kings by your shining radiance.*

Here is the first basic consideration: The kingdom which God had been promising was never meant to be centripetal, pulling all things into itself, subjecting all peoples to its own uses and purposes. Worldly kingdoms do that; self-aggrandizement is the original sin of all government, and in modern times nationalism encourages a people to think of all human issues in terms of their own interests and advantages. No nation escapes that tight magnetism; certainly not our own.

The Chosen People sometimes misunderstood and sometimes forgot that the kingdom is not meant to draw all things into itself, to serve its own interests. While we are on the point, we have candidly to confess along with Vatican II, that so has the church sometimes misunderstood and sometimes forgot.

God never forgot. The Reign of God would not be centripetal in any way. God's reign is centrifugal, flowing out from the Center and coming out from the Source. God acts this way, immensely generous, *for he causes his sun to rise on bad men as well as good, and his rain to fall on honest and dishonest men alike.* And certainly, God's Son acted this way, to the very end, for *he did not cling to his equality with God, but emptied himself to assume the condition of a slave and became as men are.*

Until the Son appeared, the people did not have clear how fully the promised kingdom was to be for others. With Jesus' ministry, it became plain that all peoples on earth were to be invited to share not only the benefits of the peaceable kingdom, but full membership in it. All of humankind were destined to stand among the chosen people. For with the dawning of the star of Jesus Christ, each person is now born into a world order that transcends anything we might have invented or even dreamed of on our own. This world order begins the secret project God has launched, and God means that the order shall draw every single woman and man into the eternal life of Jesus Christ.

This is precisely the meaning of Matthew's story of the magi and the star. It is precisely what Paul proclaimed: *In Christ Jesus the Gentiles are now coheirs with the Jews, members of the same body and sharers of the promise through the preaching of the Gospel.*

This *preaching of the Gospel* is the key, and raises the second consideration: The church now does for the nations what Jesus Himself did; as the Father had sent Him, so Jesus sent us.

Now, we are no more entirely clear about how God's secret project is working out than the Chosen People were about the earlier covenant. Paul told the Ephesians that they knew *God's secret plan,* but Paul is not around for us to question on some difficult topics. Are the kingdom of God and the church the same? How can the kingdom be split among divided churches? If Jesus is the light of the world, how can His followers rest while millions follow Buddha? If the wisdom of Christ so opposes the leaven of worldly wisdom, how can those whose only course is to live honestly in worldly wisdom come to be saved? There are lots of things that we do not know.

There are some that we surely do know. The church carries the promise. Through the living Word of Scripture and through the tradition—

particularly the sacred acts of the sacraments and the memory of the Lord's Supper, which we continually enact—Christ lives on in His church. So if *the Gentiles* find Jesus Christ, they will have followed the star of His church.

The Gentiles have not always had reason to rejoice at seeing that star, to understate the matter. The church—this is the whole church, not just the bishops and the popes—has at various epochs during the centuries made it difficult and even impossible for some nations to hear the invitation to be *members of the same body and sharers of the promise.*

For a long time, which ended not many decades ago, Christians seem to have believed not only that the hierarchical church was coextensive with the kingdom, but that the kingdom was centripetal. The church had to pull everything into itself. So the church zealously monitored (and where possible, managed) human cultures and histories, believing that the Good News gave us perspective to judge right now all human laws and governments. Where Christians had the power and thought it useful, they would simply supplant a people's culture and customs and even suppress the people's history.

We are more modest now, which raises the third point. Christians have begun to comprehend that as a church we are to share the kenosis, the "pouring out," of our Lord Jesus Christ. The church must pour out any earthly pretensions to power and governance among nations. Even as popes travel and bishops fulminate and leaders organize base communities, the church does not pretend to impose on the nations its political and social theory. We are impelled only to labor for and to give witness to what we believe and hope is true.

The church is not the arbiter among conflicting political ideologies, which take the place of idols in our day. The church does not itself have the powerful weapon of an ideology; it can only press home the interests of freedom and justice, and particularly of the marginated and dispossessed. The church serves—this is the way Christians "pour ourselves out" in imitation of Jesus Christ—serves everyone by *doing the truth lovingly* in each and every nation where it can.

In some ways this is quite simple. Where anyone thirsts, Christians offer water, mindful of the extraordinarily stern language the Master used about thirst—and about hunger, nakedness, imprisonment, and homelessness. Like the Master, we are not serving an ideology, we are serving needy people, who are always about, needing service. We promptly identify ourselves as the concerned neighbor of anyone who needs anything we have or can get. That seems simple enough.

In some other ways, spreading the kingdom is confoundingly difficult. Every word we speak represents an interpretation, some kind of assessment of the nation and its people whom we serve. When any Christians try to give witness to justice, they must do it in a web of political forces and social interests. And of course, in just about every nation and on just about any topic, Christians fall out on every side. What service of justice stands transparently for Jesus' sake, without taint of political self-interest? What claim of preaching the pure Gospel turns out to be unassailable, without taint of party or ideology to the right or to the left? Is it even reasonable to talk about a mission for the church in establishing the kingdom?

Yet, it is. Here is the third of the basic considerations. For this mission does not depend on Christians identifying the correct issues and choosing exactly the correct stance on every political, social, and economic question. We do not have to vote right in order to announce Good News. Just as well.

The mission of Christ's followers is to incarnate in themselves—now, in such wise as to be known by their works—the desires and yearnings that underlie the Commandments and the Sermon on the Mount, and that flow from the gifts of the Holy Spirit. This is how we will enact God's secret project of desire. This is how we are to be the light of the world and the salt of the earth.

Nothing would prevent a conservative follower of Christ from giving evidence of living out of those desires. Nothing would prevent a liberal follower of Christ, either. The truth is, just as *in Christ is neither Jew nor Greek, slave nor free,* so in Christ is neither liberal nor conservative, neither socialist nor laborite—but only those who have *put on the mind of*

Christ Jesus and manifest in whatever they do a passionate love for God and for those whom God creates. Whatever kind of life we are leading, we are summoned to let the Spirit of God raise the desires and yearnings in us that lead to the living of the Commandments and the Sermon on the Mount.

These desires and yearnings rise from the deepest levels of our humanity. They are closest to the passionately creative love of God our Creator, which works busily at the core of our being to call us constantly from chaos and nothingness into life and light. These desires and yearnings are the purest reflections of the desires and yearnings of God the almighty Maker. What are they?

They are beautiful and most attractive desires and yearnings, and we already know them. The desire to love maturely and to be loved. The desire to share whatever gifts we might have with all whom we love, and the yearning to accept what they have to share with us. The desire that every child, woman, and man shall have all that they need to live according to their great dignity. The desire that my neighborhood, city, and nation organize its social system and its economy in such a way that no one goes without shelter and food and medical attention, and everyone has whatever helps they need to reach their fullest education. The desire to live gently, kindly, peaceably, meekly. The desire not only to say nothing damning or carping about another, but not even to hear any such thing. The desire to do great things, to do a great work for the Lord particularly if God alone knows how great the work is. The yearning to love God above all, and all things in God.

Seeing the incarnation of these desires in Jesus' name, the nations will come to know what they are to desire and yearn for. They will find these desires and yearnings almost impossibly beautiful, even when they see them incarnate. Not quite impossibly: Notice how many secular international groups have invited Mother Theresa of Calcutta to share her desiring with them. Note how keen is the interest of the secular press in what Pope John Paul II gives witness to. How millions listened to Dorothy Day. And admired Archbishop Oscar Romero.

ment of this Power will be to raise deep in our selves the effective desires and yearnings for the Reign of God. This Power will wipe away not only every tear, but also every error, so that each one of us will desire from our whole selves the very things that God has known all along will make us eternally happy, each one and all of us together.

This is God's secret project in desire. If we let the Holy Spirit teach us in our own hearts, we will make a community of covenanted peoples whose lives are transparently good. We will manifest the One *in whom we live and move and have our being,* and who continues in us and through us the Light of the World.

And *seeing the star,* the peoples will be *overjoyed.*

Surely we feel justly astounded that we should find ourselves the ones chosen to go through this transmutation and give transparent witness to the rest how joyous a change it is.

If our desires and yearnings are to help those who do not know Jesus Christ come *to put on His mind* and to know what to desire, what kind of travesty must it be for the disciple of Jesus Christ live completely as a consumer, all desires shaped by the latest advertising, fashions, and fads.

What makes the splendid desire for justice and peace seem still like a pipe-dream when we have put people on the moon as two billion others simultaneously watched it happen?
